Cambridge Elements

Elements in Cognitive Linguistics
edited by
Sarah Duffy
Northumbria University
Nick Riches
Newcastle University

COGNITION AND CONSPIRACY THEORIES

Andreas Musolff
University of East Anglia

Shaftesbury Road, Cambridge CB2 8EA, United Kingdom

One Liberty Plaza, 20th Floor, New York, NY 10006, USA

477 Williamstown Road, Port Melbourne, VIC 3207, Australia

314–321, 3rd Floor, Plot 3, Splendor Forum, Jasola District Centre, New Delhi – 110025, India

103 Penang Road, #05–06/07, Visioncrest Commercial, Singapore 238467

Cambridge University Press is part of Cambridge University Press & Assessment, a department of the University of Cambridge.

We share the University's mission to contribute to society through the pursuit of education, learning and research at the highest international levels of excellence.

www.cambridge.org
Information on this title: www.cambridge.org/9781009660631

DOI: 10.1017/9781009660662

© Andreas Musolff 2025

This publication is in copyright. Subject to statutory exception and to the provisions of relevant collective licensing agreements, no reproduction of any part may take place without the written permission of Cambridge University Press & Assessment.

When citing this work, please include a reference to the DOI 10.1017/9781009660662

First published 2025

A catalogue record for this publication is available from the British Library

ISBN 978-1-009-66067-9 Hardback
ISBN 978-1-009-66063-1 Paperback
ISSN 2633-3325 (online)
ISSN 2633-3317 (print)

Cambridge University Press & Assessment has no responsibility for the persistence or accuracy of URLs for external or third-party internet websites referred to in this publication and does not guarantee that any content on such websites is, or will remain, accurate or appropriate.

For EU product safety concerns, contact us at Calle de José Abascal, 56, 1°, 28003 Madrid, Spain, or email eugpsr@cambridge.org

Cognition and Conspiracy Theories

Elements in Cognitive Linguistics

DOI: 10.1017/9781009660662
First published online: November 2025

Andreas Musolff
University of East Anglia

Author for correspondence: Andreas Musolff, a.musolff@uea.ac.uk

Abstract: This Element deals with the relationship between cognition, understood as the process of acquiring and developing knowledge, and diverse types of conspiracy theories, or "CTs." Section 1 lays the groundwork for the analysis by determining four components of narrative argumentative framing in CTs, of which the first three are constitutive for all CTs, with a fourth representing the "optional" collective action-guiding "scenario" component. Section 2 exemplifies manifestations of these components by discussing contemporary and historical "hoax" and "asserting" CTs and "empowering" CTs. Section 3 takes a cognitive-evolutionist and pragmatic view at the conditions for the "success" of CT scenarios. In conclusion, Section 4 formulates lessons for countering the effects of socially detrimental CTs by deconstructing them and by obstructing their dissemination.

Keywords: Cognition, conspiracy theory, scenario, conceptual evolution, framing

© Andreas Musolff 2025

ISBNs: 9781009660679 (HB), 9781009660631 (PB), 9781009660662 (OC)
ISSNs: 2633-3325 (online), 2633-3317 (print)

Contents

1 Introduction: What Makes Conspiracy Theories Attractive to Know?   1

2 How Do CTs Function?   9

3 What Makes CTs "Successful"?   24

4 How Can CTs Be Countered?   43

   References   54

1 Introduction: What Makes Conspiracy Theories Attractive to Know?

Conspiracy theories, or "CTs" for short, have a bad reputation – and a great appeal. Together with "fake news," they can have detrimental effects on the public's understanding of political issues, leading to confusion and delusions about important topics, especially crises and their possible solutions. On the other hand, many, if not most, people across ideological and cultural divides seem to enjoy accessing and "entertaining" CTs. This observation cannot come as a surprise, however, if we remind ourselves that much of entertainment fiction, from fairy tales to popular novel and film genres, is based on plots that include conspiracies and theories about them. Ordinarily, we assume that we can easily distinguish between indulging in fiction or speculation on the one hand and "real" knowledge that informs us about the world as it is on the other. So why does this ability seem to work poorly in the case of CTs? What makes them attractive as well as dangerous, powerful despite their being "debunked" time and again? Why doesn't our cognitive faculty, endowed as it is with a system of "epistemic vigilance" (Sperber et al. 2010: 359), "sort" plausible conspiracy suspicions from implausible ones as easily and clearly as it should?

Due to their pervasive presence in the media and their apparent sociopolitical impact, CTs have become an object of intensive research in several social science and humanities disciplines, including psychology, sociology, history, political science, philosophy, linguistics, and media and communication studies (Butter & Knight 2020b; Uscinski 2021; Demata, Zorzi & Zottola 2022; Danesi 2023; Butter et al. 2024; Maci et al. 2024). A comprehensive definition should take all of them into account. This Element does not attempt to do anything approaching such an overview; instead, it focuses on one aspect of CTs, namely their cognitive function(ing) in public discourse. It asks why and how CTs are, or at least seem, believable to such an extent that some of their believers risk their own lives and attack others on the basis of a CT as the main motive for such aggression. Other recipients consider the CTs they encounter in the media more or less plausible, ranging from stating CTs verbally in public or in private to just giving them a "like" on an internet website. When a CT is seriously challenged or disproven, this minimal endorsement gives them a loophole for denying any further commitment to it. Some recipients may be drawn to CTs for a variety of personal reasons or may have the general disposition of a "conspiracy mentality" (Dyrendal, Kennair & Bendixen 2021; Imhoff, Bertlich & Frenken 2022) and develop a stubborn loyalty to them and their propagators in public, even if they retain a shadow of a doubt privately. This wide range in the strength of and commitment to CT beliefs provides a rich field for psychological and sociological research (see, for example, van Prooijen, Klein, & Milošević Đorđević 2020; Uscinski 2021; van Prooijen & Imhoff 2022). That is not, however, the focus of this cognitive–linguistic study, which concentrates on conceptual structures observable from verbal statements. It refers only schematically to groups of *CT propagators* (i.e. inventors and disseminators) and *CT believers*, covering the whole range from fanatical, diehard adherents to people who "like" or sympathize with CTs without much commitment, perhaps just for reasons of entertainment (van Prooijen et al. 2022). This Element treats CTs as cognitive *framing* devices and, specifically, as *scenarios that connect experiences of a perceived crisis or a catastrophe with a story about a suspected conspiracy as its origin*. They thus provide a reassuring explanation for troubling experiences, which is what makes them attractive to hold onto. Belief in CTs is at the same time both a "stigmatized" (Barkun 2015) and also a privileged form of knowledge, as propagators and believers consider themselves the initiates of a "truth" that has not (yet) been revealed to the general public (Golec de Zavala, Bierwiaczonek & Ciesielski 2022). CTs imply a number of assumptions about the epistemic, ethical, and social status of that "truth" which this Element aims to elucidate and critique.

On account of this cognitive focus, questions about the logical and ontological relationships of CTs to "facts" will only be secondary here. In my view it is not the "fake" and/or logically flawed *information content* that defines CTs. Of course, CTs purport to provide information about a dangerous conspiracy, but this (pseudo-)factual content is not identical with their main function: that of providing a cognitively and emotionally reassuring account of a crisis or catastrophe, which is to say an event or state of affairs that is perceived not just as negative in some sense but as existentially threatening, like a war, an epidemic, or a terrorist attack (or the "invention" of it for some nefarious purposes, such as making a monetary profit from spreading its illusion). Insofar as a crisis or catastrophe is viewed as planned, the intentions behind it are invariably considered to be evil. As Barkun (2013: 4) states, CTs "[magnify] the power of evil" by suggesting that "nothing happens by accident," that "everything is connected," and by conveying at the same time the strangely reassuring message of "a world that is meaningful rather than arbitrary." They are always "more than the sum of their parts," so that individual factual or formulation details can be easily canceled without giving up the CT as a whole.

This latter, "reassuring" function of CTs stands in contrast to the predominant use of the term *conspiracy theory* as a "pejorative label" (Baden & Sharon 2020: 3; see also Räiikä & Ritola 2020: 56) in the media and much of academic research. CTs are regarded as deceptive narratives that are based on nonexistent or "fake" facts, logical gaps, and "unwarranted" conclusions (Coady 2018; Keeley 2018; Pigden 2018; Räiikä & Ritola, 2020; Mason 2022; Chlup 2023). The distinction between "warranted" (i.e. factually or logically valid theories about conspiracies) and "unwarranted," inherently flawed CTs is important for epistemologists (Keeley 2018: 47) but assumes a somewhat idealized concept of "theory" as always satisfying scientific or near-scientific standards. But outside academia, "theory" in its colloquial sense denotes all manner of explanatory accounts, including "speculative (esp. fanciful) view[s]" (SOED 2002, 2: 3236).

Such explanations are *not* "theories" in the scientific sense of systems of propositions based on empirically tested observations and their logical implications but at best probabilistic guesses. CTs belong in this wide field of pseudo-factual accounts and their nonscientific theory status makes most CTs impossible to falsify. On the other hand, given the collective experience of real conspiracies, CTs may well seem "plausible enough" to many people. As Butter and Knight (2020a: 4) observe, "Given the long history of secret machinations, both by and against the established order, it is … not prima facie unreasonable in particular circumstances for people to develop a theory that current events might be the result of a conspiracy behind the scenes."

The "factual" confirmation or disconfirmation of CTs is largely a matter of historical accident; that is, it is dependent on whether they are retrospectively confirmed or disconfirmed and these conclusions are widely, if not generally, accepted. There are indeed CTs that are regarded by the vast majority of historical researchers and the public as "decided." The exposure of the Holocaust as a "common-design" conspiracy of the Nazi leadership, as demonstrated (inter alia) in the 1945–1949 Nuremberg trials and the 1961 Eichmann trial, can be regarded as one – perhaps *the* most poignant – historical example of a confirmed CT (Office of the United States Chief Counsel for the Prosecution of Axis Criminality 1946; Mettraux 2008; Priemel 2016; Wittmann 2021). Likewise, Julius Caesar's assassination in 44 BC, the Gunpowder Plot to murder King James I and his Parliament in 1605, and the Watergate attack on the US Democratic Party election campaign headquarters in 1972 are commonly regarded as having been proven to be the results of conspiracies. Conversely, some CTs are viewed by most researchers and the public to be definitively disproven, such as the suspected high treason by the French officer Dreyfus in the 1890s that led to two false convictions, or the burning of the German parliament building (the Reichstag) in 1933 by the Dutch anarchist Marinus van der Lubbe. The Nazis tried, partly in vain, to have him convicted as the front man of a communist conspiracy; van der Lubbe was convicted and sentenced to death but his alleged communist collaborators were acquitted (Evans 2020: 92–93). Communists and other leftist politicians have claimed for decades that the Dutchman was the stooge of a Nazi conspiracy, arguing from a *cui bono* perspective ("whom did the catastrophe serve?") in view of the Nazis' exploitation of the arson attack as a pretense for introducing dictatorial rule without ever providing reliable proof (Evans 2020: 94–119). Both cases were regarded by many observers at the time as plausible CTs and were settled only decades later: for Dreyfus through a rehabilitation in 1906, and in Lubbe's case through a posthumous pardon after seventy-five years (*Deutsche Welle* 2008; Whyte 2008: 317, 432).

If we try to apply the "proven–disproven" distinction as a criterion to distinguish good "theories about conspiracies" from flawed "CTs" in an absolute sense, however, we will find it difficult to account for the changes in their epistemic status before and after their "settlement" as proven or disproven. Proven cases would then change their status from open, unresolved "CTs" to true theories about conspiracies, whereas CTs that were disconfirmed later would change their status from being a mere "CT" to a proven non-conspiracy theory. This seeming epistemic difficulty is, however, the effect of a confusion between two levels of representation in utterances. Utterances involving CTs usually involve two representational levels: (1) a content level ("crisis X was caused by conspiracy Y") and (2) an explicit or implicit epistemic evaluation level ("I believe that …" or "It has been shown/proven that …").

This nesting of representations is typical for quotations, allusions, or echoing utterances that "metarepresent" a primary representation (Sperber 2000b; Wilson 2000). The question of "factual truth" in CTs can in principle be applied to both levels of representation (causal link: level 1; proven-ness: level 2), but in its ordinary usage it only concerns the metarepresentation (i.e. level 2). The latter's truth value may change in relation to its reception and acceptance depending on the conditions of its public utterance. It does not change the relationship of level 1 content ("Y caused X") with empirically observable evidence. Any talk of a "CT having been proven" is thus a shorthand expression for a positive evaluation (level 2) of its epistemic status as an utterance in a historically situated discourse community – that is, *not* in itself an "objective truth." To illustrate the distinction, we may consider the so-called flat-earthers, who endorse a CT that a conspiracy of atheists withholds the "ancient truth" of a disc-shaped flat earth from the public and who go to great lengths to reinterpret all evidence of a spherical shape of the earth to suit their CT (Garwood 2007). What makes their views a CT is *not* the factual claim, which is of course incorrect according to near-universal scientific consensus, but the (metarepresentational) denunciation of that consensus as a conspiracy.

In contrast to cases of CTs that have been agreed by (almost) all to be proven or disproven, the vast majority have remained unresolved or undecided and have been debated to this day as *possibly* being true or false. For example, to name just one famous case, the CTs about US President John F. Kennedy's assassination in Dallas in 1963. As in the Reichstag arson case there was an immediately apprehended primary culprit, the shooter L. H. Oswald, but from the start he was suspected as acting on behalf of a conspiracy – which was, however, never discovered (Knight 2007; Gagné 2022). Let's assume, as a thought experiment, that one of the many CTs (which name, inter alia, the USSR and its Secret Service, the KGB, but also the US Secret Services, Kennedy's Vice President Lyndon B. Johnson, Cuban exiles, the Cuban government, and/or the mafia as conspirators) was unexpectedly confirmed by radically new evidence that put it beyond reasonable doubt. In this case, that particular CT version would have to be reinterpreted as a "proven" theory about a real conspiracy; all the other CTs on this topic would have to be considered falsified, as well as the "Oswald-as-lone-shooter" non-conspiracy theory. Again, that reassessment does not change the CT's "factual" truth; it only changes its metarepresentation.

Then there are cases of fantastic stories resembling the science fiction genre, including those about "alien abductions" or extraterrestrial creatures intervening in human affairs, usually with disastrous consequences (Barkun 2013: 79–157). From a commonsense point of view it seems impossible for them to be proven correct, so they may be considered fictional or delusional (Levy 2024). But that still does not invalidate them *as CTs* because they do what all CTs do: They tell a story asserting the existence of a link between a perceived crisis or catastrophe and an underlying secret conspiracy. Their fundamental unverifiability is thus *not* their defining feature; rather, it is a corollary of the modern disbelief in supernatural forces. Again, the pejorative import of the label "CT" does not concern their "theory" status but their metarepresentational evaluation.

Rather than sorting CTs into "warranted" and "unwarranted" theories, this account views them as ranging over a continuum from less to more plausible cases.

It therefore seems to me best to use the label "CT" as a generic term for *all* forms of knowledge ("theory" in the colloquial sense) about conspiracies, regardless of whether they are or have been at some point reassessed as being proven or falsified, (un)warranted, or unverifiable in principle. Even a once fully stigmatized CT may at a later point be shown to be plausible. Most of the CTs that we will encounter in this Element are, however, flawed in terms of factual evidence and/or logical stringency, but our focus is not on those flaws. Instead, this Element aims to elucidate their apparent *strengths* and their resulting *success* in integrating crisis experiences into a conceptual whole or "frame" that convinces its believers that it is more or less self-evident, such that they defend its truth as a matter of personal identity, even if it entails endangering their own and other people's lives.

1.1 Frames and Scenarios

Such conceptual wholes are called *frames* in cognitive linguistics, a generic label for "the knowledge network[s] linking the multiple domains associated with a given linguistic form" (Taylor 1995: 87; see also Fillmore 1985; Lakoff 1987, 1993; Entman 1993; Brugman & Burgers 2018). This cognitive sense of *framing* differs from its colloquial and polemically charged sense of *framing someone (up)* as falsely implicating an innocent person in a criminal activity (SOED 2002, 1: 1026). Every successful act of sense-making "conceptual integration" (Fauconnier & Turner 2002: 126) involves framing. It is of special importance in areas of public discourse that aim at achieving persuasion, for example as a technique of convincing others of the "pressing relevance of certain political facts ... by using frames in which those facts actually make sense" (Lakoff & Wehling 2016: 75). Frame analysis also underlies "Conceptual Metaphor Theory," which views metaphors as the linking of two (or more) different domains through "understanding and experiencing one kind of thing in terms of another" (Lakoff & Johnson 1980: 5). An explicit CT utterance (such as "The present crisis or catastrophe X is the outcome of a conspiracy Y") is not a metaphor but it, too, links several conceptual domains, namely those of *crisis/catastrophe* and *conspiracy*, through a supposed causal link. Insofar as the *conspiracy* aspect is expressed or suggested figuratively – for instance, as a war of an evil cabal to achieve world domination (which we will encounter in several CTs discussed later) – it does of course contain metaphors. Marcel Danesi (2023) rightly speaks of CTs as "false narratives based on underlying metaphorical constructs" and of "layers of metaphors that are mapped onto conspiracy theories" (Danesi 2023: 9, 50).

Frame analysis is thus well suited as an overarching framework for analyzing *all* instances of conceptual "mapping" (Lakoff 1993) or "blending" (Fauconnier & Turner 2002). To study CTs, however, it seems useful to distinguish them as a specific subtype of frames, specifically as emotionally loaded and pragmatically forceful or emphatic *scenarios*. *Scenarios* are a complex and dynamic type of frame that includes more than a basic event schema (source–path–goal), its participants, and their ontological relations (Lakoff 1987: 284–287; Taylor 1995: 87–90; Musolff 2016: 25–38). In addition to these basic semantic components, scenarios have narrative and argumentative structure; they contain mini-stories with a default outcome as a preferred "solution" and suggest strongly evaluative and emotion/action-guiding inferences. They are never neutral but lend themselves to polemical exploitation.

The motivation to speak of conspiracy theories specifically as *scenarios* is twofold. In the first place, the term *scenario* is meant to remind us of the story lines, scripts, and plots of theater and film dramas; that is, of explicit plans for how the story/narrative unfolds, who plays which roles, and how their actions contribute to the outcome/ending. Crucially, as social constructs that are specific to particular cultures, scenarios have a default narrative structure, which includes stereotypical characters (heroes, villains, victims …) as participants as well as stereotypical action and event sequences and a standard outcome (e.g. a "happy ending" in fairy tales) against which a nonstandard outcome stands out as an exception. As stories, they are changeable and adaptable to expectations of the respective audiences. Secondly, there is the concept of *best-* and *worst-case scenarios*, which are often presented as alternative options for decision-making processes. Thus, a highly risky enterprise is often discussed by planners in terms of a choice between different scenarios in order to aid the decision-finding process with a view to achieving an optimal outcome for the task to be completed (Yoe 2019). The CT turns this decision-finding process on its head by interpreting a perceived crisis or catastrophe as being a point at which the *worst-case* outcome has almost been reached and can only be avoided or prevented at the last minute by exposing the conspiracy behind it (Fichtelberg 2006; Zwierlein & de Graaf 2013; van Prooijen & Douglas 2017). The interpretation of a crisis as the *intended* outcome of a conspiracy thus provides a *worst-case scenario*, which is no longer merely optional. The CT scenario excludes all other, less dramatic options and demands an urgent "solution."

Such a scenario analysis focuses on CTs' cognitive function of emphatic framing, including the "maximum impact" case of empowering believers to engage in activism including violence against others and even self-sacrifice. The overall conceptual structure of CT scenarios includes three core components that form a narrative with (pseudo-)argumentative import, plus a further, politically most dangerous, *practical application* component:

(1) the (pseudo-)premise: an assertion of a presently occurring or looming crisis or catastrophe (e.g. a pandemic, a lost war, or a spectacular crime such as a terrorist attack or an assassination) or a scandalizing suspicion of its invention as a "hoax" (which the CT negates);
(2) the backstory: a narrative, explanatory account of a supposed causation of the crisis by a conspiracy with hitherto hidden motives and plans;
(3) the (pseudo-)conclusion: the circular (i.e. logically fallacious) inference that the crisis or catastrophe self-evidently "proves" the backstory and that any critic of this proof is acting irrationally and is most probably part of the conspiracy; and
(4) the resistance fight scenario: a perspective of "resolving" the crisis or catastrophe by collectively "fighting back" against those supposedly responsible for it.

In terms of its rhetorical presentation, a CT may be monological but it is always at least implicitly addressed at an audience that it is meant to persuade. It is not only persuasive in the general sense of being designed to attract as many believers as possible, but also in the emphatic sense of convincing them that they are sharing privileged, secret knowledge. This "special knowledge" aspect makes CTs seem not only useful but also enjoyable as an advantage over others. In popular culture and in literature, this aesthetic and emotional advantage can generate emotions such as feelings of superiority and *Schadenfreude*, but also compassion, through dramatic irony, which enables the spectator or reader to know the background plot better than the characters (Korthals Altes 2008: 262). Films and online games (Aupers 2020: 475) employ CTs to generate the equivalent of such dramatic irony – their "suspense" factor lies in the gradual exposure of the villain's dastardly plans, which the hero(ine) understands in full only just at the ending but which are discernible to the spectator/game player earlier on. This dramatic irony adds to the emotional appeal and enjoyment of narratives and provides a powerful cognitive asset to CTs.

Another user-friendly aspect of CTs is the wide range of epistemic commitments that they allow – that is, the degree of belief invested in them, which ranges from near-indifferent to fanatical. CTs can thus be epistemically almost noncommittal whilst still ludically appealing. They often also take the form of pseudo-naive queries and "just asking questions" (Byford 2011: 90–92), of challenges to alleged taboo topics ("asking the questions you are not allowed to ask"), or of "playing the devil's advocate" (see Section 2.3). Typical formulations in these suggested CTs are brimful with caveats and hedges ("perhaps," "possible," "why not?," "isn't it possible that ...?") which make them almost impossible to refute. They enable the speaker (and the hearer/reader) to withdraw, if challenged, from the epistemic commitment to any specific detail and present it merely as a tentative or hypothetical speculation that may need further investigation. On the other hand, some CT propagators and believers stake their own lives or livelihoods – and risk those of others – on the absolute "truth" of their narratives, sometimes with suicidal or murderous consequences, as in the case of people believing that the whole COVID-19 pandemic was a hoax. I will first focus on this *pandemic-as-hoax* CT in Section 2.1 and use examples of pandemic-related CTs later on, as they are still "in living memory," but in addition other contemporary and historical CTs will be discussed to support and illustrate the analyses. This Element does not, however, try to give a comprehensive overview of CTs (for global COVID-19 CTs see Butter & Knight 2023) but will concentrate on a set of recurring examples to elucidate the three main research questions:

- How do CTs work?
- What makes them successful?
- What are the promising counterstrategies to combat their detrimental sociopolitical consequences?

Accordingly, we will proceed in the following steps: Section 2 provides an overview of CTs (as narrative–argumentative scenarios) and their framing functions, Section 3 applies theories of conceptual evolution and metarepresentation to them, and Section 4 discusses the chances and limits of debunking CTs in view of the results of their cognitive analysis.

2 How Do CTs Function?

This section is divided into three subsections, each depicting one main type of CTs. It cuts across various typologies that have been proposed before, such as *warranted* vs. *unwarranted* (Keeley 2018: 53–57), *pathological* vs. *normal(ized)* (Butter & Knight 2020b: 29), and *event* vs. *systemic* CTs (Barkun 2013: 6). These distinctions are important but fall outside the cognitive focus of this Element. The first type of CTs to be discussed here are minimal CTs that cover just the first two levels outlined in the introduction (i.e. a crisis *premise* linked to a conspiracy *backstory*, as exemplified by so-called "hoax" CTs). The second type includes fully asserted CTs that draw explicit conclusions about the causal link *Conspiracy → Crisis*. Lastly, I will discuss the cognitively and pragmatically most compelling type of CTs: namely, "fight" scenarios that motivate believers to engage in active resistance against a perceived oppressor.

2.1 Hoax CTs, or "the Pandemic Crisis Has Been Invented"

When in January, 2020 the World Health Organization (WHO) issued a global alert about a new virus disease that was spreading from China (WHO 2020a, 2020b), the announcement was almost immediately denounced in a number of CTs as a "hoax," invented to scare the US public into compliant behavior and to effect an economic slowdown that would damage the reelection chances of the incumbent President Donald J. Trump (Imhoff & Lamberty 2020; Cook & Choi 2020). The term "hoax" (perhaps derived from *hocus*, as in "hocus-pocus") indicates an act of willful deception (SOED 2002, 1: 1250). It has been used to dismiss numerous scientific insights and achievements, such as the analysis of climate change (supposedly invented to ruin the global Western economy), the 1969 moon landing (alleged to have been staged in a film studio to secure funding for NASA), and vaccination legislation and campaigns (denounced as fake therapies invented by doctors and "Big Pharma" to make profits) (Kitta 2012; Lewandowsky, Oberauer & Gignac 2013; Jolley, Mari & Douglas 2020: 235–237). CTs which claim that something is a hoax (i.e. does not exist in reality) have a conceptual structure of two cognitive tiers: (1) a claim that the public has received misleading information and (2) the suspicion that a malicious conspiracy is behind it. It is, so to speak, a minimal or abridged conspiracy theory, because it lacks the third tier (a circular "conclusion").

Hoax CTs are, however, not restricted to science-based claims but include historical denialism, as in Holocaust denial by Nazi apologists (Guttenplan 2001; King 2017; Lipstadt 2017); Trump's denial of his own defeat in the 2020 presidential election (Baker & Glasser 2022: 549–582), which inspired the storming of the US Capitol on January 6, 2021; or the claim that the 2012 massacre of twenty-six children and adults at the

Sandy Hook Elementary School in Connecticut, USA, never took place, which led some of its believers to abuse and attack the murdered children's parents and helpers (Nelson 2013). Despite their minimalist conceptual structure, hoax CTs demonstrate in a nutshell a feature that is characteristic of all CTs. They reject the "official" information as disseminated by mass media, government agencies, and academic/scientific institutions, which is accepted by most people as a matter of course. Statements and directives of scientifically qualified medical authorities concerning illnesses, for instance, are normally accepted bona fide both on a personal and a collective basis by large majorities of people. When doctors tell you that your health and life are threatened by an illness and that a certain range of therapies are available to cure or mitigate it, normally competent adult patients will follow their advice. In the case of COVID-19, the huge number of fatalities (7.1 million over four years, see WHO 2024) and the widely known suffering of many more people would seem to make the claim that the pandemic is/was a hoax preposterous. How and why should anybody want to "invent" a pandemic? People doubting its reality and severity at the start of the pandemic may have had the excuse of lacking experience, but the first global wave in spring 2020 (which already caused hundreds of thousands of fatalities) should have sufficed to end the notion that it was a hoax. Instead, this conceit still persists in the public realm today, with fanatical believers denying its deadly effect even on their deathbed (Kale 2021; Saner 2021; Brumfiel 2022). Why is it, then, that people believe in a hoax CT to the point of self-destruction? The CT pretends to be based on evidence that contradicts the official, scientifically legitimated information, which is denounced as propaganda that serves ulterior motives. To develop and believe such a construct, one must have a suspicion to start with – for example, a conviction bordering on paranoia (Hofstadter 1964) and maintaining that there are conspirators who have invented a chimerical pseudo-disease to serve their own interests.

In cognitive terms, this suspicion provided the *frame* in which pieces of public information and personal experiences of the pandemic could be integrated. As a result, a coherent narrative was built up that lacked, however, any prima facie evidence to support it. This evidence was, however, seemingly supplied by CT propagators' suggestions in the media that the official news about the pandemic (e.g. testing results, fatality statistics) was exaggerated, while "alternative" news about easily accessible and successful cures was suppressed, and that further supporting evidence was being or would shortly be uncovered that proved complicity between scientists, businesses, and foreign powers (e.g. China) that amounted to a conspiracy. The fact that none of this supportive "evidence" has ever been substantiated has done little to stop the CT from being spread. In fact, even critical media and other public voices inadvertently reiterated it by spending a huge amount of work into its fact-checking and fake-news-debunking – that is, treating the CT suggestions *as if* they were serious factual statements. In so doing, they managed to explain to the public some of the complexities of the new virus, but what they were not able to prevent was the spread of the suspicion narrative, which remained unfalsifiable. For while it was difficult for the hoax-CT propagators to prove the nonexistence of a set of supposed hoax facts, a counterproof of the falsity of the primary hoax claim, when integrated into a CT, was also impossible. After all, the core content of a CT includes two items – crisis and conspiracy – the latter of which is based on speculative suspicion. CT holders could easily cancel some of their evidential claims concerning the crisis in question while still asserting and even widening their conspiracy claims, for example by involving alternative culprits in diverse combinations (e.g. in COVID-19 hoax CTs: US Democrats, global liberal elites, communist China, the "Big Pharma" industry complex, or rogue scientists; see Birchall & Knight 2023: 66–91). Thus, the suspicion of a conspiracy could be maintained thanks to its endless adaptability even if detailed factual claims had to be ditched. This principal non-falsifiability characterizes all CTs. Even if CT propagators are exposed as liars or frauds and publicly proven wrong, they can hardly ever be brought to acknowledge the absurdity of their claims. At most, disgraced CT propagators such as the historian David Irving (publicly exposed and convicted for Holocaust denial) or the internet influencer Alex Jones (ordered by a US court to pay compensation for the Sandy Hook massacre denial) have "excused" themselves by claiming to have been misunderstood (see Section 2.3) and by blaming critics as being members of the respective conspiracy.

Hoax CTs express a disdain for the "social construction of reality" (Berger & Luckmann 1991) by assuming that the background assumptions that are taken for granted in understanding our world are a fraudulently and malevolently invented fiction. If we cannot rely on science to identify a pandemic, on mainstream news to report a Moon landing or on election results, or on historical research to record a genocide or the attempt to storm a parliament, the boundaries between reality and imagination become blurred and ultimately irrelevant. Such a condition is a fascinating topic for philosophy or for the theory of poetry and narratology (Baudrillard 1991; Norris 1992; Rajewsky 2020), but for public communication it poses a fundamental problem. Public discourse relies on the distinction between fact and fiction in order to function. Of course, it also includes diverse, even opposing *opinions* and *ideologies*, but they all concern the same social reality and assume that there is in principle a reliable interpretation of that reality that can be shared by all. Public discourse becomes meaningless if its participants concede that the opposite of what they consider real may also be the case.

The principal challenge of hoax CTs to this commonsense view of reality lies in their tacit or explicit assumption that all or most of the normally accepted knowledge in a particular domain is fake, not just individual pieces of information. Thus, the CT of the COVID-19 pandemic as a hoax implies the assumption that all the mainstream media (as well as all governmental and medical institutions) are lying about the pandemic, its fatalities, and its biological causes, and that all people who believe their information (i.e. the vast majority of the population in any one country or even across the whole world) are dupes of a gigantic conspiracy. For such a vast suspicion to be plausible, one also has to assume enormous secret powers on the part of the conspirators to control and deceive societies. The CT believers' supposedly new, alternative insight thus consists in considerably more than learning a few new facts or questioning some old ones; rather it is akin to the religious revelation of converts or an awakening that matches "taking the red pill" in the 1999 film *The Matrix*, which allows its takers to leave the simulated world that they had regarded as normal and to "go down the rabbit hole," exploring the reality outside the "Matrix" (Wagner & Flannery-Dailey 2005).

The belief in a hoax CT fundamentally affects its holder's intellectual commitment and emotional attachment to their living world. It disarms the "linguistic division of labor" which the philosopher Hilary Putnam postulated in his essay "The Meaning of Meaning." With regard to the commonsense acceptance of differences in expertise about the meanings of everyday terms such as *gold*, Putnam observed that "everyone to whom gold is important for any reason has to acquire the word 'gold'; but he does not have to acquire the *method of recognizing* if something is or is not gold. He can rely on a special subclass of speakers … who know how to tell if some metal is really gold or not" (Putnam 1975: 145). If lay users with a nonscientific understanding of *gold* find themselves in a situation where their knowledge of its true meaning is challenged, they defer to an expert, that is, a chemist or metallurgist, to check whether an object in the real world is truly a referent of that term (Putnam 1975: 143–145). Despite the fact that scientific and other experts' unquestioned authority has suffered a relative decline in public reputation over the past decades

(Nichols 2017), most adult people are aware of the fact that they have to rely on experts who know the theories and procedures of how to determine correct from incorrect statements about most topics. One would assume that such practical epistemic deference would apply in the COVID-19 medical emergency, if only because the topical terms such as *pandemic*, *infection*, *immunity*, *virus*, and so on clearly have specialized scientific meanings. Indeed, the vast majority of laypeople did leave it to scientists and public health authorities to explain what was happening during the pandemic and what measures were needed to defend against it. The fast-rising numbers of people falling ill and dying underlined the urgency and necessity of medical experts dealing with the emergency. But to those who regarded it as a hoax, their "authority"-based information was nothing but an elaborate system of make believe. As a consequence, they did not feel obliged to follow the officially recommended protective measures such as social distancing, wearing face masks, or lockdowns.

Psychological research has confirmed that the belief in COVID-19-as-a-hoax CTs was linked to diminished risk-perception and increased noncompliant behavior (Imhoff & Lamberty 2020; Marinthe et al. 2020). Despite being minimal CTs in the sense of including only the conspiracy suspicion and a (negated) crisis account, hoax CTs have devastating consequences in that they entice people to mistrust in principle any "mainstream" information on both public health and socioeconomic/political developments and to abdicate realistic risk-assessment in their personal lives. Instead, hoax CT believers become dependent on "trending" alternative news in the media, especially in social media, which leaves them at the mercy of internet "echo chambers" and "influencers" (Evanega et al. 2020; Keith 2022; Bondi & Sanna 2022).

2.2 Asserting CTs, or "the Crisis Is Real and Caused by a Conspiracy"

If hoax CTs are based on the supposed "revelation" that a crisis or catastrophe did *not* take place because it was or could have been invented (by a conspiracy), asserting CTs insist on the catastrophe "with a vengeance," namely by insisting that it *must be* the result of a malevolent conspiracy. The most prominent asserting CT associated with COVID-19 was the narrative that the pandemic was indeed a real medical emergency but caused in a completely different way from the one told in scientific and other official statements. Instead of assuming that the outbreak was caused by an accidental animal–human crossover, it claimed that a manmade virus from the virology laboratory in Wuhan was released and then infected humans (see e.g. Kennedy 2023; Paul 2023; Smith, B. 2023; for the conspiracist internet video series "Plandemic," see Ohlheiser 2020; Lee et al. 2023). This so-called "lab-leak" account is often treated in the media as being a CT in its own right (e.g. Buranyi 2021; Stack 2023; Smith, D. 2023).

Strictly speaking, however, a statement that the virus came from a laboratory is just one of several possible factual hypotheses about the pandemic's origin. Whether it is correct or not is a matter for empirical investigation, which so far has been inconclusive, not least due to severe access limitations for international researchers imposed by Chinese authorities in Wuhan (Maxmen & Mallapaty 2021). At the start of the pandemic, when relatively little was known about its principal agent (the "SARS-CoV-2" virus), various hypotheses about its possible origin were in competition (Baier & Re 2020; Rincon 2020; Koley & Dhole 2021: 35). There was, for instance, an alternative Wuhan-linked CT with a similar ideological orientation of blaming China, which had considerable success in the first pandemic phase (i.e. that 5G broadband technology, first trialed near Wuhan and then built up across other regions in China and later globally, was causing COVID-19 [Bruns, Harrington & Hurcombe 2020]). Scientific research into the genetic structure of SARS-CoV-2 has failed to produce evidence for the "lab-leak" origin and has instead produced data that make a species crossover at a Wuhan animal market seem the most probable origin (Mallapaty 2023; Gallagher 2024).

As research on SARS-CoV-2 is ongoing and the "lab-leak" hypothesis has not been fully falsified so far, its status as false/"fake" (or, on the contrary, as truthful) information is as yet undecided. But, as argued in the introduction, the factual evidence for or against it does not determine its status as a CT. Only a narrative alleging that the production was intentional and that the leak of the virus was covered up makes the hypothesis part of a CT. This "lab-leak"-based CT includes as *frame participants* more than just a few "rogue scientists," but also the communist Chinese government, the WHO leadership (for refusing to condemn or sanction China), and scientists, politicians, and public health administrators in the West who allegedly helped to cover up the whole operation. For US Republicans, the "usual suspects" were: the Democratic Party and other political adversaries of President Trump, and all Trump-critical media. An unexpected, almost paradoxical, suspect was Dr Anthony Fauci, the Director of the US National Institute of Allergy and Infectious Diseases (NIAID) and chief presidential advisor on COVID-19. His recommendations guided much of the national and international response to the pandemic. According to CT propagators, Fauci had cooperated with the Wuhan laboratory in producing the SARS-CoV-2 virus and tried to cover up this collaboration and the lab-leak event itself (for a detailed analysis of the CT-campaign against Fauci, see Section 2.3).

Further support for the China–WHO–Fauci conspiracy was said to come from big industrial and financial institutions, headed by super-rich figures such as the Microsoft founder Bill Gates and financier George Soros, who were accused of plotting to erect a dictatorship founded on population control (Birchall & Knight 2023: 10, 59, 96, 109–110). Being based in the USA, figures like Fauci were seen as traitors "on the inside." Globally extended versions of the CT have also linked the lab leak narrative to larger and longstanding myths, such as anti-Jewish and anti-Muslim CTs, and to *superconspiracy* theories (i.e. combinations of *event* and *systemic* CTs [Barkun 2013: 6]), some of which predate the pandemic, like the so-called "QAnon"-denunciations of a "Deep State" left-wing pedophile network in the USA (the network was "revealed" over several years by a supposed military operative under the pseudonym "Q" on internet platforms; Forberg 2021; Rothschild 2021; Holoyda 2022). Another super-conspiracy is the suspected plan for a *Great Reset* of world economies to monopolize power in the hands of a global elite, or the *Great Replacement* of "white" populations by people from the Global South in Europe and the USA (Slobodian 2020; Önnerfors 2021; Holoyda 2022; Birchall & Knight 2023: 61, 86–89, 99–100). These already-globalized CTs were all "updated" with the "Plandemic"/"lab-leak"-based CT about COVID-19, which thus became a confirmation of sorts for the QAnon, Great Reset, and Great Replacement (super-)CTs. Outside the USA (e.g. in Russia and China), ideologically "reversed" CT versions alleged lab leaks from secret US-linked laboratories in Ukraine, which were then cited to justify Russia's military aggression against Ukraine (Ling 2022; Loh 2022).

This technique of integrating a specific CT within a wider "super-CT" frame will be discussed in detail in Section 3 as a main factor in making CTs successful. In terms of its cognitive function, it extends the CT's narrative, leading towards the pseudo-conclusion that an initial suspicion about unclear facts is connected with a suspected specific conspiracy (e.g. China has engineered and released the virus), which is then linked to an even wider, even global *superconspiracy*. These nested suspicions provide the "smoke" that indicates for CT believers the existence of the conspiracy "fire" that must surely be its origin. But neither factual details such as the "lab-leak" nor the suspicion frame have been proven: Both are only *potentially* true. The conclusion is therefore circular and fallacious; the facts that are supposed to prove the conspiracy suspicions are only seen as evidence *because of* the suspicions – without them they do not prove anything. If they remain unsubstantiated (as is so far the case for the "lab-leak" hypothesis), the conspiracy suspicion is wholly speculative. Even if the factual hypothesis were discovered to be true, the conspiracy itself would have to be substantiated independently to make any sense. Super-CTs only inflate the basic CT-fallacy by promising "further" evidence to be uncovered at some future point in time.

Asserting CTs in History

CTs that contain the core components of *crisis narrative, (asserting) conspiracy backstory*, and *circular conclusion* make up the bulk of well-known CTs in the last decades. They include, for instance, the conspiracist explanations for the allegedly stolen presidential election victory for Donald Trump in 2020, blamed on traitorous Deep State officials, corrupt judges, and "fake media" (Allain et al. 2023; Hall Jamieson, Levendusky & Pasek 2023); the September 11 attack on the US World Trade Center in New York and the Pentagon in 2001, "explained" as a fabrication of the US government to legitimize military interventions in the Middle East (Meyssan 2002; Wood & Douglas 2013); and the 1963 assassination of President J.F. Kennedy. At the beginning of the twentieth century, the most (in)famous CT text was the *Protocols of the Elders of Zion*, published in Russia before World War I (1914–18). This forgery purported to represent the minutes of a (fictitious) secret meeting of powerful Jewish leaders at the (real) First Zionist Congress in 1897 and sketched a plan to use these leaders' political and economic powers to subjugate the whole world under a Jewish dictatorship (Bronner 2000; Hagemeister 2022: 1–15). In Germany, where the *Protocols* were published first in 1920, they were cited as evidence for the allegation that a Jewish conspiracy had brought about World War I, financially profited from it, and sabotaged a near-certain German victory by "stabbing" its army "in the back" through strikes and other revolutionary activities (Cohn 1967: 126–148; Evans 2020: 47–83). Core motifs of the *Protocols* – such as the notion of a Jewish "international finance" elite that controls world politics – still appear in present-day super-CTs such as the QAnon and the Great Replacement myths (Wong 2020; Langer 2021; Önnerfors 2021).

In the decade leading up to the publication of the *Protocols*, the French Republic witnessed extreme polarization on account of the Dreyfus CT, in which the military and administrative establishment and right-wing political forces falsely accused the officer Alfred Dreyfus of having betrayed his country by sharing military secrets with Imperial Germany, on the basis of forged documents. After the discovery of exonerating material the conspiracists formed a conspiracy theory of their own to denounce their critics as conspirators and thus preserve the false conviction (Hyman 2005; Schultheiss 2012). Foreshadowing trends of CTs in twentieth- and twenty-first-century media, Dreyfus' defenders, who included famous authors such as Emile Zola and Anatole France, were themselves denounced as traitors and conspiracists, acting for a "vast Jewish syndicate" (Schultheiss 2012: 195) until his final acquittal after nearly twelve years (Brown 2010). Again, we see here the "extension" technique of spinning a CT further: The false suspicion against Dreyfus was not retracted when it became evident that his first conviction was a miscarriage of justice; instead, the CT propagators widened their conspiracy suspicions against more and more individuals and groups, ever suggesting new revelations and maintaining this never-ending anti-Semitic rumor far beyond his acquittal (Arendt 1973: 91–95).

Many CTs predating the nineteenth and twentieth centuries also include all three core components. These include the "blood libel" against Jewish communities going back to the twelfth century, which accused them of abusing and murdering Christian children to use their blood in the performance of religious rituals (Dundes 1991; Israeli 2017); the persecution of "witches" who were accused of conspiring with the Devil and each other to harm Christian society during the fifteenth to eighteenth centuries (Levack 2013a; Hofhuis 2022); and the allegations against Enlightenment groups such as the "Illuminati" society and Freemasons as being responsible for the 1789 French Revolution and further revolutions (Oberhauser 2020). In all these cases, the CTs rely on the fallacious circular conclusion that their respective conspiracy narrative was proven by the facts of the crisis or catastrophe that it was supposed to "explain" in the first place. In many cases, additional "evidence" was procured by forcing admissions of guilt and the naming of further suspects under torture or by forgeries. Thus, the argumentative necessity to somehow back up their allegations led CT propagators to produce post hoc the very evidence which they claimed triggered their suspicion in the first place.

How utterly arbitrarily and, in a way, creatively the supposed supporting evidence of a CT could be produced is exemplified by the recycling of a specifically anti-Semitic CT in the larger frame of the "stabbing-in-the-back" CT in post-1918 Germany. During World War I, German ultranationalists propagated the suspicion that Jewish Germans "shirked" active war service. The allegations were powerful enough to prompt the

German War Ministry in 1916 to initiate a census of Jewish frontline soldiers (Rosenthal 2007; Evans 2020: 70–72). Its results showed that Jewish Germans were as well represented as the rest of society and thus contradicted the anti-Jewish suspicion – but instead of leading to a rejection of the CT, these findings were suppressed and not published during the war. Afterwards, this non-publication was reinterpreted by believers of the "stab-in-the-back" myth as retrospective proof that their suspicions must have been correct, apparently on the absurd premise that the army's leadership had tried to shield the Jews from justified criticism. Thus, even the nonavailability of evidence could be counted as proof for the CT, rendering the pretense of a rational, fact-based argumentation meaningless.

A further type of "supporting evidence" for asserting CTs is provided by adding "complementary" hoax CTs that decry the official explanations of manifest catastrophes, such as assassinations, terrorist attacks, or putsch-attempts. The catastrophic events are thus denounced as hoaxes or "false flag" attacks that have been supposedly committed *on the orders* of the apparent victims (i.e. state authorities or establishment institutions). Examples are the Reichstag arson (as being supposedly ordered by the Nazis in the view of communist CTs, see preceding discussion), the Watergate break-in at the US Democratic Party's election headquarters (as supposedly ordered by the Democratic Party to incriminate Nixon; see Jolley, Mari & Douglas 2020: 232), the 9/11 attack (as supposedly ordered by the US administration under President G. W. Bush to provide a pretense to launch wars in the Middle East), or the 2016 coup attempt in Turkey (as having been "staged" by the incumbent government of President Erdogan in order to discredit the opposition; see Lusher 2016). These "supporting" hoax CTs need not even be particularly plausible in themselves, but they seemingly "round off" or complete the main CT of a conspiracy-cum-further cover-up, thus reinforcing their believers' impression that none of the official and mainstream media information can be trusted. The alleged conspirators are accorded an almost superhuman foresight and omniscience, as they are supposed not only to have planned the conspiracy and the crisis of catastrophe as its result, but also to have designed an official explanation to cover their tracks (which the CT believers "know" to be a hoax).

Framing Trumps Argumentation

Asserting CTs are the products of a framing strategy that *simulates* narratively an argument from premises, based on objective evidence and leading to a logically valid conclusion. Their backstory of a conspiracy (which is truly no more than a suspicion) is assumed to be proven by the manifest crisis/catastrophe and only needs "further corroboration." The CT supplies its own "proof" by generating its own criteria for finding and deciding what counts as evidence. This circular and self-justifying character of CTs has long been noted and denounced as fallacious and misleading (Keeley 2018: 54–57; Baden & Sharon 2020; Birchall & Knight 2024). From the perspective of "pragma-dialectical" argumentation theory (van Eemeren & Grootendorst 1992; van Eemeren & Houtlosser 2002), CTs can be seen as examples of fallacious "maneuvering" regarding the "burden of proof" because they deny the validity of all counterargumentation and base their conclusions only on evidence that has been preselected to suit them. That is, in colloquial parlance, they are instances of *begging the question* or *conclusion shopping* (Walton 2008; Butler 2020).

While the possibility of criticism is a crucial component in any valid argumentation that follows the ideal of "domination-free discussion" (Habermas 1972: 233), it is usually dismissed as irrelevant by CT-holders on the grounds that they already are in possession of privileged, secret knowledge and are not fooled by mainstream media or epistemic authorities such as official administrators, politicians, or scientists. The latter's counterarguments are viewed as irrational rejections of a self-evident truth and signs of naivety and gullibility – or, in the case of outspoken critics, of their bad faith and participation in the conspiracy. As a result, Putnam's principle of the "linguistic division of labor" is overridden in asserting CTs, just as it was in the case of hoax CTs: Any deference to CT-critical "expertise" is seen as a surrender to the conspiracy. This characteristic makes CTs particularly attractive to populist movements and politicians (Bergman & Butter 2020). In the case of COVID-19-related CTs, for instance, populist politicians such as the Presidents D. Trump in the USA, J. Bolsonaro in Brazil, and A. Lukashenko in Belarus took a thinly veiled anti-science stance as "men of the people" who stood up to global administrative and scientific elites, not just by questioning their authority but also by accusing them of self-interested conspiracies (Kakisina, Indhiarti & Al Fajri 2022; Weiss 2023).

2.3 Empowering CTs, or "Our Resistance Proves the Existence of the Conspiracy"

The breakthrough of developing and launching vaccination programs against COVID-19 in late 2020 (Krammer 2020; Li et al. 2020) stopped the uncontrolled spread of the pandemic but it did not stop the creation of new conspiracy theories and their public dissemination. On the contrary, the introduction and rollout of the vaccines soon triggered further CTs and led to a rise in noncompliant behavior, specifically via rejecting vaccination (Hotez 2021a). The motivations were diverse, building on already extant CTs (e.g. that the vaccination was completely superfluous because the pandemic itself was a mere hoax, or that the vaccine was designed to make people even more ill). But they went far beyond such vague general concerns, alleging specific conspiratorial designs such as the vaccination being a cover for the implementation of microchips to track and/or mind-control individuals and groups or stigmatize them with the apocalyptic "mark of the beast" (Inwood & Zappavigna 2022). These anti-vaccination CTs must not be confused with scientific or clinical concerns about side-effects and failures of vaccines for particular groups of patients (Ledford 2021a, 2021b). News about vaccinations that did not work and led to dangerous, in some cases deadly, side-effects was, however, exploited and exaggerated by CT propagators to foster vaccination-skepticism and resistance, which they complemented by narratives about corrupt scientists acting for "Big Pharma," as well as powerful individuals such as Bill Gates or George Soros, foreign powers, and/or global elites (Langer 2021; Pertwee, Simas & Larson 2022; Birchall & Knight 2023).

CT propagators also recycled longstanding CTs and religious beliefs about *all* vaccinations functioning as attacks on the health and sanctity of the human body (Bok, Martin & Lee 2002) and linked them to traditions of skepticism towards public welfare and healthcare systems in general, especially among so-called "prepper" groups that took pride in their supposed "self-reliance." They had indulged in noncompliant behavior already in the early phase of the pandemic (e.g. by refusing to obey social distancing rules and wearing face-masks), but the principal rejection of vaccination was of a different quality. It signaled a determination to *not* accept the healthcare provision supplied by national and international health authorities and to actively *resist* its implementation. As a result, verbal and violent physical attacks on health officials increased (Hotez 2021b, 2023; National Academies of Sciences, Engineering, and Medicine 2023). The resulting additional pressure of undecided patients impacted hospitals, care homes, and health systems, to the point of health workers having to deal with patients dying from COVID-19 while rejecting available treatment (*Modern Healthcare* 2021). Scientists, already vilified as traitors, were now denounced as *murderers*, which justified in the eyes of some CT-believers violent attacks on them and even killing them (Nogrady 2021, 2024). How could CTs motivate this extreme degree of destructive activism?

The same question has been asked about infamous historical CTs that were linked to catastrophic world-historical crises such as wars and genocides. The Holocaust or "Shoah" – the murder of six million Jewish people in Europe at the hands of the Nazis – has been explicitly connected, for example, with the conspiracy outlined in the *Protocols of the Elders of Zion*. Some historians have claimed that the *Protocols* text was a "warrant," "blueprint," or "license" for the Jewish genocide (Cohn 1967; Wippermann 2007: 67–77; Wistrich 2010: 158). The case for this judgement may seem open and shut, given that leading Nazis such as Hitler, Goebbels, and Rosenberg endorsed the *Protocols* (Rosenberg 1923; Hitler 2016: 799; Goebbels 1993, II, vol. 8: 287). However, as Evans (2020: 28–29) has pointed out, referencing these endorsements begs the question of whether the *Protocols* really informed or motivated Nazi policy.

Only one far-right terrorist group in the Weimar Republic seems to have been directly motivated by the *Protocols*: the assassins of the terrorist "Organisation Consul" who murdered the Jewish German Foreign Minister Walther Rathenau as an alleged member of the "Elders of Zion" in 1922 (Evans 2020: 27). The "identification" of Rathenau as one those "Elders" was, like the whole supposed conspiracy, completely fictitious. The Nazis retrospectively expressed their sympathy for the assassins but that does not prove a contemporary parallel belief in the *Protocols* in 1922. Nor did the *Protocols* text contain any of the main Nazi allegations of an innate tendency of a Jewish "racial parasite" to destroy the German nation or the Aryan race (Bein 1965; Musolff 2010: 24–42). Hitler, Goebbels, and other Nazi leaders were well aware of the fact that the authenticity of the *Protocols* was in doubt early on (Bytwerk 2015: 212–215), so it is not plausible that it was the basis for their plans for genocide ideology. Rather, the *Protocols*' "revelations" about Jewish plans for a world dictatorship were "taken by the Nazis to confirm what they already knew" (Evans 2020: 45) – that is, as a corroboration from an outside source "to legitimate anti-Jewish legislation and persecution" (Girard 2020: 571) – and it served them as a point of reference in their propaganda. A *blueprint* for the Holocaust they were not.

The "blueprint" metaphor for the *Protocols* is more plausible in the sense of providing a textual summary or *frame* for the whole range of suspicions against Jews that had grown up in the second part of the nineteenth century, the popularity of which the Nazis relied on. The frame was easily adaptable to any new crisis or emergency that could somehow be linked to suspected Jewish culprits. It had existed in many countries since before the publication of the *Protocols* and it lived on despite its exposure as a forgery. In post-1918 Germany, nationalists blamed their country's defeat in WWI on a whole sequence of alleged Jewish-led conspiracies, all of which fitted the *Protocols* frame: (1) an alleged "encirclement" of Germany by the *Entente*-powers France, Britain, and Russia, organized by Jewish financiers (Krumeich 1989), (2) the sabotage and cowardice of Jews during the war allegedly proven by the aforementioned 1916 "Jewish census" of the German army, and (3) the specific "stab-in-the-back" narrative of a Jewish-led cabal who thwarted Germany's near-certain victory and engineered the "shameful" armistice of 1918 and the Peace Treaty of 1919 (Krumeich 2019; Evans 2020: 70–83).

Each of these treason narratives can be analyzed as a CT "in its own right" but together they form a series of ever more radical and general applications of the super-CT frame of the "perennial" (Hagemeister 2022) suspicion against Jews, which was adapted to successive experiences of crises and catastrophes in the master-narrative of eternal Jewish guilt. This series culminated in Hitler's 1939 "prophecy" of the "extermination of the Jewish Race" as a revenge for "plunging the nations once more into a World War" (Hitler 1965: 1058). Hitler's "prophecy" that the Jews deserved extermination as punishment for their alleged conspiracy against the whole world – and especially against the German people – was supposed to be fulfilled by the Holocaust (Evans 2005: 604–605; Herf 2006: 52–53). As post-WWII history has shown, however, the anti-Semitic super-CT of a Jewish conspiracy to achieve world domination has retained the power to generate new narratives about conspiracies that need to be resisted far beyond Europe. New CT propagators, such as the terrorist organization Hamas in Gaza, harken back to the *Protocols* as supposedly reliable evidence for a Jewish conspiracy to destroy the Palestinian people by erecting the state of Israel (Simonsen 2020: 364–367). Again, it would be wrong to assume that the *Protocols* originally "inspired" this new twenty-first-century anti-Semitism; rather, the reference to them is recycled to bolster new CTs, like the idea that Israel's existence is a product of preplanned Western Jewish colonialist/imperialist conspiracies that must be resisted (Webman 2011; Hoffman 2023). As the murderous attack of Hamas against Israel on October 7, 2023 showed, the CT is virulent enough to embolden its holders to engage in murderous – and to some extent suicidal – violence (Sachs 2023). In such an extreme case, the identity of being a resistance fighter, and the readiness to risk one's own existence for that identity, is seen and experienced as the ultimate "proof" of the CT.

In addition to the question of how CTs are able to motivate their believers to (self-)destructive activism, we must also ask how this motivation, as a cognitive-emotive effect, can apparently "survive" over longer periods of time and spread across different cultural contexts, despite sustained campaigns of debunking them and despite repeated historical experiences of the CTs' catastrophic consequences. This rather depressing "success" of CTs to turn into super-narratives that survive their own falsification is the focus of the following section.

3 What Makes CTs "Successful"?

Given the power of CTs to "inspire" their adherents to violent, deadly actions against others and suicidal actions against themselves, it is tempting to focus on their trigger function for such catastrophic consequences at the expense of the analysis of their "positive" appeal to believers. How can CTs with potentially catastrophic social consequences become attractive to so many people in a particular cultural or temporal context, while observers outside that context find the CTs risible and their consequences disastrous? This section aims to explain the apparent "fit" between CTs and the sociocultural environment in which they are created and disseminated by taking a cognitive-evolutionist perspective.

This perspective refers to the neo-Darwinian approaches to cultural history that have developed since the 1970s. In analogy to Darwin's understanding of biological evolution, they assume a "blind" process of selection and reproduction (Dawkins 1976, 1999, 2004; Blackmore 1999; Aunger 2000). As the cultural counterpart of the biological replicator (the gene), Dawkins proposed the neologism *meme* as a "unit of cultural inheritance" that is "selected by virtue of its 'phenotypic' consequences on its own survival and replication in the cultural environment" (Dawkins 1999: 297). Like genes, memes can be analyzed as unconsciously "selfish" agents of their own evolution, that is, as adapting to their respective environments by way of natural selection from random mutations. This gene–meme analogy is not, however, straightforward. Sperber (1996, 2000a) has pointed out that the evolution of memes, as representations of concepts, is not determined only by the need to survive and propagate but that it depends on the continuous interpretive transformation of "mental" into "public representations" and vice versa. Its "evolution" can then be seen as a tendency towards the production of "contents that require lesser mental effort and provide greater cognitive effects" and are communicatively more "relevant" than others (Sperber 1996: 53). The innovation rate in meme replication is much higher than in the standard model of genetic mutation, which likens meme evolution, in Sperber's view, to that of viruses (Sperber 1996: 25, 102–104). This view has led to the pejorative metaphor of socially and/or ethically "bad" memes as *mind-viruses* (Brodie 1996; Dawkins 2004), which may indeed also be an apt metaphor for many CTs.

W. Croft and D. A. Cruse have adopted the neo-Darwinian, "naturalist" approach to analyze the historical development of languages, in particular for outlining the "evolution" of metaphors (Croft 2000; Croft & Cruse 2004). Croft proposes a "two-step" model in which all meaningful elements of utterances, including metaphors, are viewed as *replicators* whose conceptual evolution is a function of semantic "innovation," on the one hand, and "entrenchment" in socio-communicative contexts, on the other (Croft 2000: 23–29). Diachronic variation of metaphors, for instance, is understood as a product of the interplay between semantic creations and their sociolinguistic entrenchment and dissemination. If we combine this two-step model with Sperber's insight into the relevance-driven mutual (re-)interpretation process inherent in every act of communication (from mental to public representation and vice versa), it becomes evident that metaphorical innovation occurs all the time: Semantically new memes can be embedded in and adapted to a familiar (that is, speaker–hearer-shared) sociocultural environment; or familiar, already-established memes are transferred across diverse new sociocultural environments. This general model of conceptual innovation can be employed in the analysis of CT evolution. In the following section we will exemplify this approach for two cases: first by discussing its use in the analysis of the witchcraft CTs that haunted Europe for several centuries (as a long-term CT) and then by investigating the more recent (and hopefully also more short-lived) emergence of a "local" variation of COVID-19-related CTs in Germany in 2020.

3.1 CTs as "Selfish" Memes: The Evolution of Conspiracist Scenarios

One of the most longstanding historical CTs was the belief in "witches" who allegedly conspired with the Devil and among themselves to harm individuals, whole communities, and their worldly and spiritual authorities in Europe and America, spanning a period from the late fourteenth to the late eighteenth century (Cohn 1975, Levack 2006, 2013a; beyond the European-American sphere, there is of course a global anthropological and theological dimension to the belief in demons and witches). The European CT complex based on belief in witches certainly deserved Barkun's (2013) label of a super-CT but did not form a static, homogeneous system. Originating from medieval theories about the pervasive presence of demonic powers in the world, the witch CT complex acquired distinctive conceptual innovations over the course of the Renaissance and early modern times, including beliefs that witches could influence the weather, climate, and nature; that they could shapeshift into other bodies; that they congregated as groups ("witches' sabbaths") and could magically fly. Also part of this complex was the identification of their "familiars" and, fatefully, their prosecutors' acceptance of – and indeed preference for – physical torture to obtain confessions at all cost. The introduction of torture in interrogating "witches" at first necessitated explicit ideological justifications, but once introduced, it quasi-automatically multiplied the number of suspects and confirmed the belief in witches through apparently conclusive confessions and testimonies (de Blécourt 2013; Hofhuis 2022: 161–172). Following dramatic episodic and local upsurges in "witch hunts" in the late seventeenth century, which threatened the cohesion and existence of the respective communities, the enormity of the persecutions led finally to growing official and popular resistance (Hofhuis 2022: 173–178).

This new sociocultural environment in turn provided a context in which the judicial, scientific, and religious counterarguments that had been leveled against witch-hunts since their beginnings gained credence (Levack 2013b; Hofhuis 2022: 310–316), leading to the further problematization of beliefs in witches. In the eighteenth century, a core concept of witch CTs (i.e. their key function of "fighting the Devil," which had dominated religious discourses) became more and more irrelevant in the increasingly secularized and science-dominated cultural environments in Europe and North America (Elmer 2013a, 2013b). As a consequence – albeit gradually and with significant regional differences – "witch-persecutions went extinct" (Hofhuis & Boudry 2019: 24). Since then, over the course of the last two centuries, the religious legitimation of witch CTs has effectively ceased and witchcraft beliefs have been recategorized as irrational "superstitions" that supposedly exist only among marginal groups in Western societies and/or in non-Western cultures (Evans-Pritchard 1950; Douglas 1970; Rabo 2020). Nevertheless, motifs of witchcraft CT beliefs keep resurfacing to this day in suspicions of Satanism and ritual child abuse that feed into present-day CTs (whilst the term *witch hunt* itself has been reinterpreted as a metaphor for the persecution of innocent victims; see Ayto 2010: 386). One example of recycled secularized witch CTs is the so-called "Pizzagate" CT that started circulating on the internet in 2016, according to which a criminal ring of US "liberals" had children abducted and held in underground prisons. These children, the CT alleged, could be ordered by the conspirators under the cover of pizza deliveries and subjected to sexual abuse or the "harvesting" their blood and their (supposedly mind-enhancing and/or life-extending) adrenaline derivative adrenochrome (Bloom & Moskalenko 2021; Holoyda 2022). The Pizzagate CT led to violent threats against the alleged conspirators and a gunman's attack on a pizza restaurant in Washington (Thalmann 2019; Miller 2021). It is thus debatable whether we should view witch CTs as a past historical phenomenon that "our" modern society has overcome or recognize in the Pizzagate story a new version of the old witch CT mind-virus.

The variation in witchcraft CTs across historical periods, regions, and national cultures is reflected also in the diversity of historical explanations of their supposed "real" motivations (e.g. discrimination against minority groups, suppression of women, resistance to state and church elites, and attempts to resolve inner-community tensions; Levack 2006: 175–202; Hofhuis 2022: 184–204). The "cultural Darwinian" perspective, in contrast to approaches that arbitrarily prioritize one explanation over others, accommodates such variation by following a "selfish culture hypothesis" (Hofhuis 2022: 210). This hypothesis assumes that those "cultural variants that accidentally enhanced the reproduction of the witch-hunts were selected and accumulated" in their respective regional and period contexts (Hofhuis & Boudry 2019). It focuses on the details of changes in the popularity and virulence of witch CTs and relates them to a "thick" description of the communities in which they temporarily flourished (Hofhuis 2022: 358). In terms of the neo-Darwinian approach, witch CTs can be seen as narrative meme-complexes that were successful when and where they could serve as cognitive scenarios to explain and overcome natural, economic, and social crises and catastrophes such as (civil) wars, epidemics, or starvation caused by bad harvests. In competition with other available crisis narratives, the witch CTs must have been more attractive to believe in, offering as they did a seemingly plausible "solution" to the local crisis through the persecution and punishment of the individuals and groups stigmatized as witches. The witch CT complex thus became a self-perpetuating, changing narrative meme that gained the quality of a self-fulfilling promise: If the crisis experiences persisted, more witches had to be found and persecuted until the crisis came to a socially satisfactory conclusion in the eyes of believers. The well publicized falsifications of witch allegations by CT critics were insufficient in stopping the witch hunts as long as they fulfilled that function in the respective communities, especially where church and state authorities still backed them tacitly (Levack 2013b). Until then, they still engendered conceptually innovative witch CT variants that responded to the perceived needs of local communities.

By comparison with the super-CT of witch beliefs, which stretches over more than three centuries, COVID-19-related CTs can only be accorded a "micro-evolution" since their inception in 2020. Still, their conceptual variation and their transcultural spread also invite a cognitive-evolutionist approach along the lines sketched above for witch CTs. The devastating impacts of the COVID-19 CTs on specific communities can be viewed in analogy to the "upsurges" of witch hunts. Pandemic-related CTs that interpreted COVID-19 as a hoax, as a hostile national attack, or as an attempt for global population control (see Section 1) provided "backup" arguments for the deaths of patients who refused COVID-19-specific treatments (*Modern Healthcare* 2021; Keith 2022) and for patients' self-damaging use of "alternative" cures recommended by influencers and politicians (Birchall & Knight 2023: 94–96). CT-based resistance against the social containment measures and vaccination campaigns to halt the pandemic also led to violent – in some cases, fatal – attacks on medical staff, social workers, and members of the public (Hall Jamieson 2021; Pentucci 2022; US Attorney's Office 2022; National Academies of Sciences, Engineering, and Medicine 2023) and to attacks on Chinese and Asian-looking people due to "China virus" CTs (Wang & Catalano 2022). These CTs led to enduring public confusion over scientific statistics concerning fatality figures, infections, vaccinations, and patients suffering from "long COVID" (Lewiński & Abreu 2022; Hotez 2023; Marshal 2023). The CTs were "backed up" by the argument that the rise in infection cases was the result of increased testing rather than reflecting the spread of the pandemic. Despite the refutation of this simplistic conclusion by experts in mathematical statistics, speculations about an artificially fabricated inflation of data about the pandemic persisted for years (Begley 2020; Jarvis 2022).

These detrimental effects of COVID-19-related CTs spread globally as fast as the pandemic itself, despite the efforts of many governments, media, and supranational organizations such as the WHO to shield the public from them (Wodak 2021; Holland & Jarvis 2024). From an evolutionist perspective, we can regard the various pandemic CTs and their sub-versions as memetic CT narratives within a "globalized" super-CT complex, undergoing continuous replication/reinterpretation and competing for maximum dissemination. We can then ask how these *global* pandemic CTs became culturally *localized* into scenarios that motivated their believers to take violent action and risk harm to themselves and others within their sociocultural context. (This concept of *localization* is drawn from theories of translation and intercultural communication, where it captures the adaptation of texts and products to a local sociocultural context, as a counterpart to the corresponding notion of *globalization*; see e.g. Coupland 2010). In the remainder of this section we look at the spread of such an "innovative" COVID-19-related CT variant in Germany.

On August 29, 2020, the German capital Berlin witnessed a large protest rally against the government's COVID-19 restrictions, which by that time had already included social distancing, mask mandates, and lockdowns (one in spring 2020, and another one expected for the following autumn and winter). The demonstrators (who numbered around 40,000 according to police estimates) comprised a multitude of protesters from across the whole political spectrum, ranging from loosely organized groups of "independent" or "lateral thinkers" (*Querdenker*) to advocates of "alternative" lifestyles (including "New Age" science skeptics) and far-right groups (Pantenburg, Reichardt & Sepp 2021; Reichardt 2021). This wide variety of groups from all political/ideological corners should not be interpreted as evidence for a truly spontaneous, grassroots character of the rally. On the contrary: Sociological research has shown that "the protest organizers follow[ed] a strategic logic" (Plümper, Neumayer & Pfaff 2021: 2247). During the afternoon of August 29, one of the right-wing protest groups, about 400 strong, broke through the barriers around the Parliament building, the Reichstag, and ran up its stairs with the ostensive intention to get inside, spurred on by rumors that the police would stand aside and the bizarre notion that US President Trump had come to Berlin to help them personally (*Der Tagesspiegel* 2020; *Die Welt* 2020a, 2020b; *Die Zeit* 2020; *T-Online* 2020a, 2020b). They were, however, stopped by a small police force guarding the Reichstag, who hindered them from advancing into the building, kicking some of them down the steps to the main entrance.

This attempted "storming" of the Parliament was photographed and filmed and became a news item across the world (*The Guardian* 2020; *The New York Times* 2020). It soon became clear that the group that had attempted the "Reichstag storming" consisted mainly of so-called "Reich citizens" (German: *Reichsbürger*), that is, extreme right-wing opponents of the present-day German state, the Federal Republic of Germany (FRG). These Reich citizens usually refuse to pay taxes or other official fees (Pentucci 2022: 20). Some Reich citizen groups have taken on fantasy patriotic names such as "United Patriots" (*Vereinte Patrioten*), "United German Peoples and Tribes" (*Geeinte Deutsche Völker und Stämme*), or "Free State Prussia" (*Freistaat Preußen*), but they are closely interconnected (Schönberger & Schönberger 2023). They have existed in Germany since the 1980s, but have grown in size, especially after the 1990 unification in conjunction with other right-wing groups, including the far-right party "Alternative for Germany" (*Alternative für Deutschland*; AfD), which, on the basis of a strong anti-immigration stance linked to a German-specific version of the Great Replacement CT (*Correctiv* 2024), has gained considerably in popularity over the last two decades, rising from below 5 percent share of the vote in the first national election it contested in 2013, to 20.8 percent in the 2025 national elections.

The 2020 "storming" of the Parliament, though in practical terms a failure, had a high symbolic value as a first-ever attack on the center of post-WWII German democracy in its historic building. Global media showed the demonstrators carrying flags and banners bearing the colors of the 1871–1918 "German Empire" (black, white, and red) and the symbol of its "imperial" eagle (*T-Online* 2020a, 2020b; Thorwart 2020). As the following years showed, the August 2020 action was no one-off event – it was part of a far larger political strategy. During 2021 and 2022, groups of Reich citizens were arrested and put on trial for making concrete preparations to abduct the federal health minister, Karl Lauterbach, kill the Saxon minister president Michael Kretschmer, and even lead an armed putsch against the national government (*Deutsche Welle* 2022; *Der Spiegel* 2022, 2023a, 2023b; *Die Welt* 2022, 2023; Thorwart 2022; Kupper & Dittrich 2023). By 2021, police forces in Germany already estimated their strength as at least 2,000 violent activists, including some officers from the armed forces, and 21,000 sympathizers (Pawelz 2022). For these groups, the pandemic crisis, with its potential for social and political unrest, appeared to be a fitting context in which they could launch their plans for overthrowing the hated federal state and re-found a *Reich* that could negotiate such a peace treaty as the German nation was supposedly denied after WWII (in order to keep it "enslaved" by the Western victorious powers) (Rathje 2017, 2021; Schönberger & Schönberger 2023).

But what have a far-right nationalist CT about Germany's enslavement and nostalgia for the pre-WWI empire to do with anti-COVID protests? Prima facie, a link of authoritarian ideology and healthcare protests in Germany is counterintuitive, for the 1871–1918 German empire was known for its strict policies against infectious diseases (Hess 2000; Thießen 2013). It is by no means self-evident that present-day German right-wing extremists should try to form the avant-garde of an anti-authoritarian protest rally against pandemic policies. Neither is it self-evident that the protest movement should allow itself to become fellow travelers of far-right extremists keen to engage in scuffles with riot police and to plan an overthrow of the state. However, when studying the conspiracist narratives of both sides in detail, some convergent argumentative trends emerge. On the presupposition that the government's anti-COVID-19 containment measures such as social distancing, lockdowns, mask mandates, and, ultimately, vaccination were superfluous, the authorities trying to impose them became the target of suspicion (i.e. for having hidden ulterior motives for imposing the containment measures). Noncompliance with the restrictions was likened to an act of "resistance" on a par with anti-fascist resistance during the Third Reich. Some protesters even posed as equivalents of Jewish Holocaust victims by wearing mock Star of David symbols stigmatizing themselves as untested or unvaccinated. Similarly, they denounced the COVID-19 laws as a repeat of the 1933 "Enabling Act" (*Ermächtigungsgesetz*) that had legalized the Nazi dictatorship (*Der Spiegel* 2020; *Deutsche Welle* 2020). The *Reichsbürger* CT of the German federal government acting on foreign orders to keep the nation enslaved matched their suspicions of the state authorities' hidden agenda sufficiently to join arms and legitimize using violence against it.

More details about the Reich citizens' motivation to join and spearhead the 2020 rally became known three years later when the weekly *Die Zeit* published a dossier reporting the results of a series of interviews with twenty-nine of the *Reichsbürger* demonstrators identified as participants in the attempted "storming of the Reichstag" (*Die Zeit* 2023). Their statements provide some, albeit self-reported, insights into the conspiracy beliefs that motivated these protesters to engage in their violent actions. The informants articulated two main lines of argument and shared one common emotional experience. The two arguments for excusing their actions consisted in (1) minimizing their personal actions or involvement in the violence (especially in view of the then-ongoing judicial investigation and prosecution) and (2) insisting on the legitimacy of resisting the national COVID-19 restrictions on the grounds that they were violations of their human rights and in any case the result of a colonial regime, in contrast to the last "proper" German state (i.e. the old empire founded by Bismarck, where everything was "in order") (*Die Zeit* 2023). Their shared emotional experience of the "storming" event was described as "huge joy" (*riesig gefreut*), solidarity of "us against the rest of the world" (*Wir gegen den Rest der Welt*) and being together with "so many wonderful" people (*so viele tolle Menschen kennengelernt*) (*Die Zeit* 2023). Some verbal aggression also came through in the interviews, in the form of insults against the journalists (e.g. as "prostitutes" of the ruling "system") combined with threats to prosecute or even use violence against them or against members of parliament (*Die Zeit* 2023). All in all, the 2020 rally was assessed retrospectively as an epiphany-like experience in which their long-held suspicions were revealed as true by the manifest repression of an authoritarian state. Blending their own CT narrative of an alleged national enslavement with the conspiracist criticism of COVID-19 restrictions seems to have presented the Reich citizens with a unique chance to view themselves as part of a popular uprising in self-defense, which they tried to "enact" through storming the parliament and preparing for a coup d'état.

Criticism of COVID-19 restrictions after the first lockdown by the wider civil protest movement and parts of the broader public thus presented the Reich citizen groups with a unique chance to interpret and promote their own CT scenario (national oppression) as part of a general popular uprising, which they tried to "enact" through storming the parliament and preparing a putsch. In a wider global perspective, the QAnon-inspired suspicions of a worldwide conspiracy of evil elites were concretized into the specific situation of a "battle" against the national government and its executive forces (who were thus legitimate targets for acts of resistance and counterattacks). In Barkun's (2013) terminology, such a combination of a local-nationalist CT and global COVID-19-related CTs can again be classified as a super-CT in the sense of a "supercharged," enhanced CT that urges people into violent action, in which they could validate their feelings of frustration and hostility towards the state and could enact fantasies of a people's rebellion. Remarkably, this radicalization dynamic of the CT-based "resistance fight" scenario was activated in the pandemic situation within months of the outbreak, in stark contrast to the CTs of long duration (such as witch beliefs or anti-Semitic CTs, which developed over centuries). In a comparative perspective, the microevolution of the August 2020 fight scenario at the Reichstag reveals itself as the result of a super-fast fusion or blending of CTs which, though conceptually unrelated and diverse, suddenly "made sense" together as revealing a hidden pattern behind the believers' crisis experiences and providing an opportunity for their resolution.

This "resistance fight" scenario as a fulfilment of the Reich citizens' "fight for liberation" can serve as a test case for comparative analyses of the "success" of diverse CTs in radicalizing believers, such as the 2021 storming of the Capitol in Washington, DC (combining, as it did, local – i.e. US-national – CTs implied in the "Stop the Steal" campaign with global COVID-19-related CTs [NPR/IPSOS 2020; Allain et al. 2023; Hall Jamieson, Levendusky & Pasek 2023]), and also historical CT "upsurges" such as the Dreyfus trials, specific witch hunts, anti-foreigner riots, or racist pogroms based on CTs. A central connecting characteristic of such events seems to be the believers' experience of their violent actions as epiphany-like revelations. This liberating "resistance fight" scenario fulfils both cognitively and emotively reassuring functions: It provides seemingly incontrovertible manifest "proof" that the conspiracy in question exists – namely, in the form of a concretely identifiable enemy – and it conveys an experience of solidarity among the self-appointed resisters (viz. the QAnon slogan "Where we go one we all go" see Wendling 2021).

In the evolutionist perspective, the integration of COVID-19-related CTs in the Reich citizens' national resentment CT can be analyzed as a memetic *adaptation* to a specific sociocultural environment. Conceptually, it involved the "innovative" reinterpretation of already existing COVID-19 CTs as confirmed by the Reich citizen experience of being oppressed by illegitimate, foreign-controlled rulers. In the competition with other CTs it was sufficiently "successful" to have a public breakthrough in the far-right groups' actions. Due to a number of adverse factors, not least the police action at the Reichstag in August 2020, the uncovering of their terroristic plans, and the subsequent judicial prosecutions, the propagandistic activity by Reich citizen as meme carriers has recently diminished. On the other hand, this super-CT is also almost certain to "survive" in the form of new conceptual adaptations (e.g. in the rhetorically toned-down but narratively congruent versions propagated by right-wing extremists to undermine the legitimacy of the federal government in Germany) (AfD 2020, 2022).

3.2 CTs as Scenarios with a Dissemination Dynamic of Their Own

Following the evolutionist perspective with its distinction between meme-innovation, on the one hand, and meme-dissemination, on the other hand, this section focuses on the latter aspect. It asks: How can CTs, once they have been created and put in the public sphere, "survive" in competition with each other and with mainstream, authoritative explanations of crises? As has already been argued, it is hardly their flimsy information content that makes belief in CTs attractive. Their conceptual ingredients are exchangeable, variable, and even "cancellable," depending on the propagandistic and ideological contexts in which they are propagated. Thus, for audiences of COVID-19 CTs who believed already that "white" Western culture was the victim of a "Great Replacement," the pandemic "made sense" as a means to reduce or exterminate it (Birchall & Knight 2023: 141); hence, the narrative of COVID-19 as being spread on purpose and being followed by a deadly vaccination campaign seemed for them plausible. If, on the other hand, audiences were mainly worried about "not being told the truth" by governments and scientists, the hoax version sufficed. Both CT versions could even be combined despite their mutual logical incompatibility (Bruns, Harrington & Hurcombe 2020; Imhoff & Lamberty 2020). However, beyond their integration into and with other CTs, what is it that makes certain CTs particularly attractive and thus "successful" in competition with other CTs and commonsense crisis explanations?

Whilst CTs with the same target topic may sometimes contradict each other in their details, they have one essential aspect in common: They presuppose the existence of a hidden, "true" reality behind the make-believe, misleading mainstream information – that is, its control by a conspiracy. CT believers assume they have a privileged access to this hidden reality, which entitles them (at least in their own view) to use uncooperative and fallacious forms of "strategic maneuvering" against criticism, especially concerning the "burden of proof" (van Eemeren & Houtlosser 2002). They present their own claims and conclusions as being self-evident (i.e. not needing any further proof); they also appeal to sources that are "only seemingly authoritative" (van Eemeren & Houtlosser 2002: 24), and act as if the standpoint of their critics "had been refuted" when they had not (van Eemeren & Houtlosser 2002: 25). A case in point is the routine refusal of COVID-19-CT believers to accept any substantial burden of proof. Neither the hoax-CT believers nor the vaccination skeptics engage with the overwhelming evidence of publicly available statistics of pandemic fatalities and recovery (Hotez 2023); instead, they appeal without any backup to nonscientific "authorities" such as politicians and (social) media pundits (Jennings et al. 2021; Andone & Lomelí Hernández 2022) and often simply deny counterevidence (Maxmen & Mallapaty 2021; Mallapaty 2023). Similarly, adherents of 9/11 CTs have failed to engage with the detailed proofs from the analysis of the ruins and from physical experiments showing that the affected buildings did collapse and burn down due to the impact of the airplanes flown into them (Dunbar & Reagan 2011; Bergmann 2025: 66–68). Likewise, the believers in the 1933 Reichstag fire or the Kennedy assassination CTs, who insisted that one person could not have perpetrated those crimes, have denied over decades the existence of all reliable evidence that pointed towards the solitary culprits (Evans 2020: 107–119; Gagné 2022: 72–103).

When attempting to compensate for their disengagement from material evidence for their core claims about a conspiracy, CT propagandists and believers often focus on "proving" its existence by way of circumstantial evidence, shifting the burden of proof to a seemingly more accessible terrain. QAnon believers, for instance, have had as their "database" only the cryptic messages sent by a poster under the pseudonym "Q," which they have to decipher (i.e. speculate about) for themselves in their "echo chamber." They therefore concentrate on arguing about the finer points of "Q"-exegesis, rather than finding the source or assessing the plausibility of "Q-drop" messages (Forberg 2021; Holoyda 2022; Bondi & Sanna 2022). This invitation-to-speculate is similar to that of computer games that entice their players to search endlessly for clues (Thorwart 2020). This gaming quality imparts a ludic attractiveness to CTs but it leaves believers unsatisfied for most of the time spent on their "quest." Hence, it is only in moments of a sudden epiphanic revelation, such as the attempted 2020 "storming of the Reichstag" in Berlin or the storming of the US Capitol in Washington in 2021, that the CT temporarily seems to be confirmed – specifically, through violent action. However, unless these experiences can be repeated and intensified, the quest for confirmation of the CT suspicion continues, which likens it to an addiction that never comes to a rest.

The reception history of the *Protocols of the Elders of Zion* provides a classic example of the CT believers' century-spanning quest for confirmation. The *Protocols*' dubious character as a text (i.e. in its being the product of forgery and of repeated plagiarism of anti-Semitic writings dating back to the eighteenth century) was publicly exposed as early as 1921 and was further exposed in two high-profile trials in Switzerland, which confirmed its fictitious character (Hagemeister 2022: 21–38). In Nazi Germany, where the *Protocols* were emphatically endorsed by the Nazi leadership as supposedly proving their suspicions against "World Jewry's" conspiracy, these publicized doubts about the published Russian texts' authenticity were well known, even to Hitler and Goebbels (see Section 2.3). After WWII, the *Protocols* were further discredited and a stream of critical research has since identified every single source of the historical plagiarisms in the text (Cohn 1967: 60–107; Hagemeister 2022: 1–20). Nevertheless, they continue to be recycled and applied (e.g. in contexts of anti-Israeli propaganda [Webman 2011; Hoffman 2023]) and in conspiracist "explanations" of COVID-19 as the product of a global elite plot (Zipperstein 2020). This continuing readaptation of *Protocols*-based CTs shows that they mainly serve the believers' search for new opportunities to see them "come true" again and again, like the prophecies of Nostradamus. Neo-Nazis and present-day terrorists denying Israel's right to exist (Landes & Katz 2011; Girard 2020) still feel entitled to attack the state of Israel, Jewish institutions, and individuals with reference to the *Protocols*, not *because* of but *regardless* of the details of the original text. In this sense, the *Protocols* are a prototypical CT "mind-virus" (Dawkins 2004) that generates, through continuing variation and adaptation, its own momentum for continued dissemination. It provides time and again a "virtual" subtext for anti-Jewish interpretations of all real-world crises that can be invoked, often indirectly or metonymically (e.g. as the dog-whistling clue to "International Finance," which is beyond critical discussion or reflection) (Subotic 2022).

Occasionally, however, CT propagandists and believers find themselves confronting critics and nonbelievers who won't take the unproven assumption of a conspiracy (or its enactment in a violent fight scenario) as sufficient proof of its truth. The following section deals with the tactics with which CT propagators and believers shield themselves – and immunize their CTs – against radical conceptual/ideological critique and competition.

3.3 Self-Justification of CT Scenarios: Immunization against Criticism

Declaring factual details of CTs irrelevant is, as we have seen, a routine defensive move of their propagators and may convince followers who are already certain that a conspiracist account of their crisis experience is right. It is, however, a weak form of "strategic maneuvering" in terms of argumentative plausibility. Of course, CT propagators can meta-communicatively deny that they have abdicated the commitment to discharging the burden of proof but in any, even minimally, open argumentation, such a move appears as an obvious fallacy that may make their stance an object of derision. To avoid such a loss of credibility, the semblance of commitment to searching for evidence must be kept up. So, how do CTs "survive" open falsification?

One set of seemingly more sophisticated tactics is to declare one's CT to be a mere hypothesis or to be meant figuratively (i.e. not as a proposition that entails strong epistemic commitments) so that those who believe its literal version appear to have misunderstood it. The concomitant loss of face is compensated by immunity from judicial prosecution. The professional CT propagator, talk show host, and internet influencer Alex Jones, for instance, employed it to defend his hoax-CT slur against the victims of the 2012 Sandy Hook Elementary School massacre, in which twenty-six people were murdered by a gunman. In his radio talks and on his internet platform InfoWars, Jones had alleged that the victims, their families, and helpers who had come to the rescue were all actors in a drill exercise who "staged" the shooting to support reforms to the liberal US gun laws (Olmsted 2023). In 2022, he was sentenced to pay $1.5 billion in compensation to the victims of his defamation, some of whom had been subsequently harassed and attacked by CT believers (Nelson 2013; Otten 2022). Apparently aiming to restore Jones's reputation and to justify his readmission on the social media platform "X," the platform's owner, Elon Musk, invited him to take back his hoax CT. On Musk's prompt, Jones was quick to assert that "of course" he had not wanted to imply such a denial but that he had only covered what others had said and thus could not be held responsible for the actions of his CT followers: "I just ... play devil's advocate ... And if that hurt people's feelings, I apologize. But I did not send people to your houses. I did not pee on graves" (Olmsted 2023).

Jones's answer includes several "minimization strategies" that turn it into a near-perfect "non-apology" (Benoit 1997; Kampf 2009): He attempts to shift responsibility by blaming others (e.g. talk show listeners), as well as by apologizing for potentially ("if") having hurt "feelings" and by claiming to have only "played the devil's advocate" (i.e. to have taken up an stance opposing the main proposition, simply in order to be evenhanded and to consider all possibilities) (Ayto 2010: 92; Pascovich 2018). This excuse presumes the existence of uncertain (i.e. still debatable) aspects of the topic. If that were the case, playing the devil's advocate would be an intellectually respectable exercise for interpreting an issue that is still unknown to some extent (van Eemeren, Houtlosser & Snoueck Henkemans 2007: 19). As some factual details of a crisis or catastrophe may remain unclear for some time, a conspiracy scenario may indeed be a potential explanation, however improbable it may be from a common-sense viewpoint. In Jones's case, however, the notion that the amply documented mass murder had not taken place was no "remote possibility" that could be considered by the *devil's advocate*. The denial only made sense as a pretense to justify the invention of a conspiracy for the supposed hoax; here, that the anti-gun lobby "staged" the school massacre to legitimize their calls for tighter gun laws. Argumentatively, it amounts to the circular (i.e. fallacious) conditional statement: "If the shooting had been invented, it would be proof of a conspiracy, therefore, let's assume that the shooting was invented."

This fudging of the boundary between documented, proven, and potential invented "facts," or, in the words of Donald Trump's PR counselor K. Conway, the presentation of "alternative facts" (Blake 2017) appears to be part of a wider "post-truth" trend (d'Ancona 2017), which aims at confusing critics by pretending to make an explanatory argument about "facts" when in reality it is the suggestion of a wildly speculative suspicion. Within a CT such as Jones's "Sandy Hook hoax," or the COVID-19-as-hoax theory, there is no fact-based "premise" that could be used to build an explanatory conclusion: Their cognitive import amounts only to a speculative conditional. The presumed conspiracy is never substantiated but used to construe new opportunities for keeping the debate open. Jones's "devil's advocate" defense amounted to no more than a hypocritical self-excuse from the real-world consequences of his own CT.

Variants of this strategy can be found in many CT propagators' self-justifications when they have been publicly exposed as relying on invented assumptions. Like the devil's advocate defense, they involve the notion of not having spoken "in earnest." Thus, when confronted with legal prosecution for their self-publicized attempt to "storm" the Reichstag in 2020 and their plans for a putsch, one of the Reich citizen defendants declared the accusation to be an "old wives' tale" (*Ammenmärchen*) (*Die Zeit* 2023; *Frankfurter Allgemeine Zeitung* 2024a, 2024b). US President Trump's incitement of his followers to march to the Capitol and "fight like hell" on January 6, 2021, to rectify the "steal" of his supposed election victory was defended by his attorney as a way of "speaking metaphorically" (*The Hill* 2021). The leader of the Dutch far-right party Forum for Democracy, Thierry Baudet, disclaimed his own denunciation of political adversaries as "reptiles" (which echoed D. Icke's notion of reptilian bloodlines controlling the world [Icke 1999)] as being "of course a metaphor" (Emmery 2022). This list could be extended further but the argumentation tactic is the same: It comes down to a partial retraction of the CT by reinterpreting it as a hypothetical "debating point." This tactic still weakens the CT's credibility but keeps it in play as an "open question" and thus maintains the "quest" character of the CT belief.

A second, more aggressive and more powerful tactic of CT propagators is the counteraccusation against CT critics or opponents that they are part of the conspiracy. Instead of abdicating or reducing the burden of proof for the CT, this one "raises the stakes," so to speak, by adding further sub-CTs to an already existing main CT. An example of such a CT-defense tactic was the vilification of Dr. Anthony Fauci, the Director of US National Institute of Allergy and Infectious Diseases (NIAID). In several COVID-19-related CTs Fauci was cast as a traitor scientist who was allegedly responsible for the pandemic by collaborating with the Chinese bioweapons laboratory in Wuhan. The Fauci-centered CTs acquired a momentum of their own, outlasting his retirement at the end of 2022, and triggered investigations and accusations in the US Senate and House of Representatives as well as in Republican-leaning media. His case can serve as an exemplary illustration of the self-perpetuating force of CTs.

Fauci's "Treason"

When the COVID-19 outbreak started, Fauci had already been the director of NIAID for eighteen years, with a high professional reputation, having led public health management responses to epidemics such as HIV/AIDS, SARS, swine flu, MERS, and Ebola (NIAID 2023). Serving under President Trump, who had gained office in 2016, and continuing under President Biden until his retirement, Fauci fielded questions at most of the Presidential press conferences on COVID-19, gave numerous interviews, and issued press releases to explain the US government's health measures, which also were seen as a model to follow in large parts of the "Western" world. In the early phase of the pandemic, in spring 2020, he was praised and cited reverentially as the "one of the nation's top infectious disease experts" (*The Washington Post* 2020a). However, as early as April 2020 death threats against Fauci emerged and necessitated police protection for him as well as a public defense of sorts by President Trump: "(Fauci) doesn't need security, everybody loves him … Besides that, they'd be in big trouble if they ever attacked." (*CNN* 2020). The background for these threats was at first mainly the pandemic-as-hoax-CT, with claims that the COVID-19 mortality figures reported by Fauci were exaggerated and that the containment measures were unnecessary (*The Washington Post* 2020a). In addition, Fauci favored the "wet market" hypothesis of the pandemic's origin (as has been discussed) and avoided endorsing Trump's preferred "lab-leak" explanation (*The Hill*, 2020; *The Washington Post* 2020b; Banco & Lippman 2021; Musolff 2022).

As the "lab-leak"-based CTs proved to be unprovable, Fauci might have seemed unassailable to his detractors. In order to "support" their suspicion against him, they developed a new sub-CT: that his obstruction against the lab-leak hypothesis served to cover up a historical cooperation between the National Institutes of Health (NIH), of which Fauci's NIAID institute was a part, and the Wuhan laboratory in so-called "gain-of-function" research (*Breitbart* 2021a, 2021b, 2023). As NIAID director and NIH board member, Fauci had been involved in authorizing cooperation that included coronavirus research in China, albeit considerably before COVID-19 (i.e. ending in 2014). When questioned by a US Senate committee, he refuted the allegation by rejecting the contentions that the Wuhan studies qualified as "gain-of-function research" and that they had produced the viruses which were responsible for the COVID-19 pandemic, pointing to genetic differences between the relevant virus types (Kessler 2021; Olmstead 2022). He thus became a prominent CT critic and opponent of the "lab-leak"-centered allegations, and despite his protestations of scientific objectivity (*National Geographic* 2021; *Newsweek* 2023), he started to be blamed for the human and socioeconomic costs of the pandemic management (Ohlheiser 2020; Lee et al. 2023). CT-propagating internet "influencers" designed a special rhyming meme for his supposed crime: "Fauci lied – millions died" (Hoft 2021; see also Hall Jamieson 2021). By late 2021, Fauci was embroiled in the US political confrontation between the Republicans, working for a future reelection of Trump, and the Democrats. His appointment as Chief Medical Advisor by the new President, Joe Biden, reinforced Republicans' suspicions that he had deliberately contributed to undermining President Trump's authority (Paun 2023) and that his explanation of the pandemic's origin was part of a conspiracy to help cover up his own cooperation with "establishment" figures and businesses (Bill Gates, "Big Pharma") and Chinese institutions (Kennedy 2021, 2023; Paul 2023). CT proponents now called for Fauci to be "ambushed," "waterboarded," or "tried and executed" for having betrayed the US, and he was compared on Fox News to the murderous SS doctor Josef Mengele from Auschwitz, infamous for sadistic experiments on Jewish children (*Newsweek* 2021; *The Washington Post* 2021; Schumaker 2023). In 2022, a Virginia man was sentenced for having sent Fauci emails stating that he and his family deserved to be "dragged into the street, beaten to death, and set on fire" for his "crimes" of treason and mass murder (US Attorney's Office 2022).

The casting of Fauci as an evil traitor scientist in COVID-19 CTs enabled their proponents to "spin" new sub-CTs that relied on ever wilder speculations about possible new evidence, which never materialized. Similarly to Alex Jones's "devil's advocate" argument about the Sandy Hook "hoax," they substituted a completely implausible account for any real evidence regarding COVID-19's origin and alleged that the latter was being hidden by Fauci himself (and further coconspirators in the scientific "establishment"). The very absence of original evidence was thus blamed on the CT's critics. In its place, the CT's propagators then presented the prospect of new circumstantial evidence that had nothing to do with the pandemic's origin itself but with Fauci's alleged clandestine and surreptitious inter-collegial communication style. Republican members of the US Congress and Senate tried to make Fauci admit in public hearings that he had tried to "suppress" the lab-leak theory in secret emails and phone calls (*USA Today* 2022; *Newsweek* 2023; *The New York Times* 2023); they even fabricated fake video material showing him breaking down in tears, admitting his supposed "guilt" (Petersen 2022; Stolberg & Mueller 2023). Their allegation of his pressure on colleagues to drop the lab-leak hypothesis contrasted starkly with the record of all his public statements (to the effect that he could not rule that hypothesis out). Equally well documented was his repeated preferred explanation of the virus (on the basis of DNA data) as "most probably" coming from a Chinese "wet market," which was by no means the glowing endorsement of Chinese virus control that one would have expected from a pro-China scientist. But all these contradictions between Fauci's public statements and their CTs did not matter to their propagators. The main goal of their never-ending allegations was, after all, not criticism of China but finding some kind of "smoking gun" proof for the existence of a "Deep State" or "Big Science" conspiracy at the heart of the US administration.

The length to which CT propagators go to find and, if need be, fabricate evidence that critics or non-CT-endorsing experts are parts of the conspiracy illustrates a further cognitive function of CTs. The CTs are thus immunized against criticism by denouncing the critics as being members of the respective conspiracy. As a world-famous scientist, Fauci could have been the most believable "crown witness" for the lab-leak-based CT had he endorsed it. His refusal to do so made him, conversely, the prime suspect – an enemy-traitor who must have a personal (pecuniary and/or political) motive for covering up the supposed truth about COVID-19's origin. The scientific reasons that he cited were deemed to be a smokescreen for his underhanded activities, as CT propagators' reiterations of ever the same speculations about his emails and phone calls in the hearings showed (Waldman 2021; Kozlov 2023, 2024).

This never-ending quest to "discover" hidden emails or other clandestine records proving Fauci's treasonous involvement in a COVID-19 conspiracy had a predecessor of sorts in the so-called "Climategate scandal" of 2009–10 about a leak of allegedly hidden emails from climate scientists at the University of East Anglia (UK) providing data for the UN's Intergovernmental Panel for Climate Change (IPCC). As in Fauci's case, this circumstantial "proof" was a substitute for the lack of primary evidence. The supposedly incriminating emails had been textually reassembled by the CT's propagators so as to make innocuous exchanges about data presentation look like self-incriminating admissions of hiding "embarrassing" data from the public, all of which turned out to be baseless (Pearce 2010; Powell 2011: 159–169; Zorzi 2022). Such long-lasting and media-feeding, but ultimately inconclusive, investigations and hearings of CT suspicions resemble the McCarthy-era search for communists in post-WWII America, in which the not-to-be found spies in the US military and administration were replaced as suspects by Hollywood actors and other artists (Gladchuk 2006).

Historically, CT critics have regularly been accused of being part of the respective conspiracies themselves. Thus, all critics of the *Protocols of the Elders of Zion* were denounced as members of the alleged Jewish conspiracy to achieve world domination, irrespective of whether they were Jewish or not (Evans 2020: 35). Critics of Dreyfus' prosecution were similarly accused as being "in the pocket" of rich and powerful Jewish elites (Schultheiss 2012: 194–195). In the days of witch CTs it was extremely risky to doubt their legitimacy, lest one wished to be implicated as a witch or sorcerer oneself, on the "testimony" of suspects who had been tortured with the purpose of making them reveal more names (Lehmann & Ulbricht 1992; Hofhuis 2022: 350).

In present-day CT debates, one new variant of this "self-defense by counteraccusation" strategy has developed. It is not quite as fatal as accusations of being an accomplice of witches during the sixteenth and seventeenth centuries, but still presents CT critics as biased, prejudiced opponents of the innocent search for truth, and conversely, the CT believers as "truth-seekers" or "truthers" who only try to ask innocent questions and suffer for doing so. This is the metapragmatic move to reject the "CT" label itself as a derogatory invention of the mainstream conspiracy (Deschrijver 2021) and of any fact-checking and -correction as an act of "debunking the truth" (Garcés-Conejos Blitvich & Lorenzo-Dus 2022). In such attempts at refuting CT criticism, the contested status of the CT serves as a (pseudo-)argument for its supposed "truth" and the CT believers' "knowledge activism" (Garcés-Conejos Blitvich & Lorenzo-Dus 2022: 95). This self-exculpating move shields the CT propagators and believers against criticism by relying on a background super-CT that casts them as the victims of slander and stigmatization. This "counter-counter-CT" was, as we have seen (Section 2.1), particularly popular with COVID-19-CT believers who styled themselves as a persecuted minority on a par with Nazi victims and as would-be "freedom fighters" against an alleged "COVID dictatorship".

4 How Can CTs Be Countered?
4.1 A Red Herring: Fact-Checking for CT Falsification

The insight that CTs cannot be effectively countered by simply supplying "facts and figures" has by now become almost a commonplace in the research literature on the evidence that many falsified CTs have persisted over longer periods of time; examples in recent decades have included the enduring CTs about the Kennedy murder, the 9/11 terrorist attack, or the COVID-19 pandemic (Barkun 2013: 158–169; d'Ancona 2017; Gagné 2022: 100–103; Birchall & Knight 2023; Bergmann 2025). Butter & Knight (2020a: 2) rightly insist that "conspiracy theories are not identical with fake news." As argued in Section 1 of this Element, fact-checking and "fake news"-exposing on its own is not a viable strategy against CTs because most of them are non-falsifiable, and the few historical CTs that appear to have been confirmed or disconfirmed by research or judicially based consensus were resolved only after many years (or even decades), so that for much of their existence in the public sphere they remained undecided. Even after a generally accepted debunking, they are usually *not* fully abandoned by their propagators or followers. Instead, as the preceding section showed, they are "argued away" through excuses such as that of the CT being only a hypothetical argument from a "devil's advocate" point of view or a metaphorical way of speaking. Moreover, as the evolutionist approach to CTs has demonstrated (see Sections 2.1 and 2.2), many present-day superconspiracies such as QAnon and the Great Replacement include sub-CTs adapted from centuries-old beliefs, such as Satanism, witch CTs, and anti-Jewish or anti-Islamic prejudice complexes. Some of these sub-CTs never seem to die out completely, like the blood libel dating back to the twelfth century which has reappeared in the Pizzagate and QAnon CTs. The feasibility of conclusively falsifying them appears to be illusory, as they have already "survived" repeated debunking attempts and fulfill apparently popular tastes, like those for occultist fiction, horror, and science fiction stories.

It must be stressed, however, that such an acknowledgement of CTs' enduring popularity does not at all invalidate their fact-checking, fact-correction, or "debunking" and factual falsification as *heuristic moves* in combatting CTs. Indeed, these and argumentative countermoves – such as highlighting their implausibility, as well as ironical subversion and "cognitive infiltration" (by turning CTs' tacitly presumed skepticism against them) (see Sunstein & Vermeule 2009; d'Ancona 2017: 129–149; Krekó 2020) – are essential tools to fight against CT "weaponization"

(Bergmann 2025). On the other hand, a preoccupation with fact-checking every sub-CT and circumstantial "evidence" claim may play into the hands of CT propagators, as it only reacts to and follows new quests for "supporting evidence" (see Section 3.3) and thus extends its public dissemination.

When we recall that CTs' central cognitive function lies in the reassurance of audiences whose confidence in having a sufficient overview of their living-world reality has been undermined by experiences of crisis or catastrophe, even such argumentative countering is unlikely to remove the fundamental conditions for the emergence and successful adaptive evolution of CTs. As far as regards the creation and emergence of CTs ("memetic innovation"), it may even be argued that it is both impossible and unnecessary to prevent. As long as humans feel helpless and disoriented by crises, their cognitive creativity will produce conspiracy scenarios that seem to make sense of an uncertain "reality" and that motivate them to engage in (political) actions to solve the crises. A few of these scenarios may even prove to be correct (i.e. conspiracies that are revealed to have taken place) and their exposure may lead to a cathartic, liberating effect. "False" CTs, on the other hand, manage to linger on and revive again and again due to their reassurance function until the latter has lost its attraction, which may take a very long time.

What then can a cognitive-evolutionist analysis contribute to developing strategies to "neutralize" CTs that go beyond factual "debunking"? On the basis of the preceding discussion, two strategies seem worth considering, namely those of (1) preventing CTs from being developed into resistance fight scenarios that promise believers a victorious outcome, and (2) obstructing the dissemination of CTs through deconstructing the never-ending quests for and presentations of supposedly new "circumstantial evidence" that extend CTs' conceptual "careers."

4.2 Combatting Scenario Formation

As argued before, CTs are "theories" in the colloquial sense of the term; that is, they are invented conceptual constructs that link a given crisis/catastrophe experience with a presumed conspiracy, for which there is no immediately obvious evidence. At this stage, a CT is not much more than a privately entertained suspicion. This privately held "mental representation" of a causal link, "Conspiracy X → Crisis Y," may spread (through verbal and multimedia communication) and become a "public representation" (Sperber 2000a), with the particular slant of contradicting an already established official narrative of the crisis. The latter is of course also an explanatory account but is deemed unsatisfactory by CT believers because it allegedly underestimates or hides the true extent of the conspiracy, for example by identifying only a single perpetrator (as in the assassination of J.F. Kennedy) or a relatively small group of perpetrators (such as al-Qaeda for the 9/11 attack); by explaining the crisis as the result of an accidental mishap (e.g. the theory of the COVID-19 origin as a chance animal-human crossover event); or by even admitting that it is not yet resolved (as in the mysterious disappearance of Malaysian Airlines flight MH370; see de Changy 2021). Against the supposedly misleading and mendacious official account, CT propagators assume a defensive position of proposing an alternative account to reveal the "real" conspiracy. This "counter-CT" may be at first a more or less plausible speculation among others, which is entertained or believed to a greater or lesser degree by its recipients, depending on their disposition for a "conspiracist mentality" (Lantian, Wood & Gjoneska 2020; van Prooijen, Klein & Milošević Đorđević 2020). Even if they are shared in an internet chat-group or in a private meeting in the real world, such nascent CTs are hardly likely to have an immediate attitude-changing and action-inspiring impact. However, their continued repetition as "privileged" knowledge within a group that views itself as being stigmatized by the official knowledge holders may well create the basis of a feeling of solidarity and cohesion among the "chosen few" who consider themselves to be "in the know" (Douglas et al. 2019: 8–10). They accord themselves the status of alternative "experts" who, instead of relying on the "division of linguistic labor" (Putnam 1975), view themselves as the only true knowledge holders – that is, the ones who should be deferred to by others. Even then, however, an isolated CT existing in a niche of the offline or online world will still not be memetically successful as long as its potential adaptive potential is not realized due to a lack of wider uptake.

The essential condition for such an uptake is the integration of a CT with other CTs and worldviews by the CT propagators into a narrative complex that appears to provide a fully coherent explanation for a set of crisis/catastrophe experiences of their audience and to outline an action scenario for them that has a positive "solution" outcome. Once construed, such a scenario can be turned into a quasi-concrete experience that seems to confirm the CT-holders' beliefs in the possibility of a final "victory." Thus, the Reich citizens managed to integrate their CT beliefs about COVID-19 (both as a hoax or fabrication) with nationalist resentments about the alleged foreign occupation of Germany sufficiently to enact the 2020 Reichstag battle (Section 2.2). A similar dynamic emerged from Trump's "Stop the Steal" CT alleging that a "Deep State" conspiracy had cheated him out of a victory in the 2020 US presidential election, which in combination with QAnon-beliefs, led to the "storming" of the Capitol on January 6, 2021. It is at this "scenario"-stage that a CT is turned into an apparently self-fulfilling prophecy that has the force to trigger an epiphany-like revelation for its holders.

It stands to reason that at moments of such seeming fulfilment of CT beliefs the commonsense "epistemic vigilance" (Sperber et al. 2010) techniques or consensus-oriented, "pragma-dialectical" argumentation strategies (van Eemeren & Grootendorst 1992) are set aside for the experience of a shared understanding of an "inner truth" about what goes on behind mainstream politics and for the emphatic optimistic feeling of overcoming it, together with one's "comrades in arms." The supply of "more facts and figures," instructions about logical thinking, or advice to believe in what official "experts" or "authorities" say are insufficient to counter this emphatic experience. The only form of cognitively effective countermeasures seems to be the deconstruction of the conspiracy scenario, for example through *persistent* questioning of its apparent coherence. It is not sufficient to rely on the one-off effect of the "better argument." Rather, a sustained exposing of a CTs' non sequiturs, false backup arguments, and overgeneralizations – together with the reassertion of consensus information – can challenge CT-holder' beliefs without damaging their socio-communicative "face" and still "update" (i.e. correct) their understanding of a crisis experience in favor of a less conspiracist explanation and even worldview (Cook, Lewandowsky & Ecker 2017; Costello, Pennycook & Rand 2024).

Deconstructing CT narratives is perhaps easier against asserted CTs than for hoax CTs, as the latter are often disguised, when challenged, as being "devil's advocate" arguments or as "merely questioning" the discrepancies in the mainstream consensus, to avoid incurring argumentative commitments. However, insofar as they assume the existence of a specific conspiracy scenario, this can be also questioned, for example by rejecting the burden of proof evasion by the CT's proponents.

After all, the principally skeptical attitude that CT believers apply to "mainstream" explanations can also be turned against their own CTs in order to break up their apparent super-coherence. Such a "subversive" approach in countering CTs is, however, only possible in contexts of roughly equal discussion rights, that is, when counterarguments are allowed to penetrate details of CTs' assertions and challenge their backup evidence. These conditions may be difficult to achieve in polarized or highly adversarial contexts, such as when scientists are publicly interrogated by CT-sympathizing politicians but not allowed to "talk back," as was the case in the media treatment of "Climategate" in the UK or in US Senate hearings on the COVID-19 pandemic management, where the burden of proof commitment was one-sidedly loaded against the scientists who were treated as a priori conspiracy suspects. On the other hand, well-conducted judicial procedures providing affordances for an evenhanded allocation of burden of proof seem to offer good chances for exposing and deconstructing the absurdity of CTs, as in the humiliation of CT propagator David Irving in his libel case against critics who had exposed him as a Holocaust denier (which was later reiterated by a conviction for that crime in an Austrian court; see Shermer & Grobman 2000 and Lipstadt 2017). The implementation of such deconstruction strategies in appropriate institutional contexts designed to expose the CT propagators' own pretended expert authority and the CTs' internal pseudo-argumentative coherence seems more promising as a means to counter CTs than a sole reliance on fact-checking and debunking. The following, final section looks at ways of obstructing CTs' uncritical dissemination.

4.3 Obstructing CT-Dissemination through Cognitive Deconstruction

The spread, or dissemination, of CTs has been researched extensively, especially with regard to the impact that internet communication and the rise of "social media" on mobile phones have had over the three past decades (Stano 2020; Mahl, Schäfer & Zeng 2022). Much of this research remains stuck, however, within the paradigm of viewing CTs as forms of disinformation or "lying." It rightly notes that CTs, like fake news and false rumors, are at first reiterated mainly *inside* the discourse niches, "bubbles," or "echo chambers" of the world wide web until their endorsements and reiterations in the form of "likes," "retweets," and "trending" threads reach a critical mass and then suddenly and quickly multiply, reaching and misinforming many millions. But that is where the similarities end. CTs are, as we have seen, conceptually and rhetorically more complex than representations of individual pieces of incorrect factual information because they connect their account of a crisis or catastrophe experiences with a conspiracy "backstory" into narrative wholes. Their purpose is not merely to spread false information but to motivate their recipients to believe in, and potentially enact, scenarios of confrontation that are supposed to resolve their cognitive-emotional "dissonance."

Whilst there seems to be little chance to prevent the emergence or invention of CTs, obstructing their spread as "mind-viruses" may be more feasible. One aspect of this strategy are legislative and administrative interventions to regulate social media providers. This aspect is beyond the remit of this analysis and requires media-sociological, educational, and technological treatment, as well as an in-depth discussion of legal and ethical implications. In the following section I will sketch perspectives for *cognitively* deconstructing CT narratives in as far as their dissemination turns them into virulent CT scenarios (i.e. platforms for activism). For this, I build on the four core components identified earlier.

Deconstructing Hoax CTs

To deconstruct hoax CTs may seem easier than it is in the face of a present or imminent crisis: At first sight, downplaying a pandemic such as COVID-19 as a bout of seasonal "flu" and denouncing the WHO's pandemic alert as scaremongering (Brooks 2020), for instance, seem too absurd to deserve sustained counter-argumentation. But in terms of crisis management, preventing a mass panic is not against common sense, and neither is a measured degree of resistance against exaggerations and hectic calls for hyper-activism by the media. However, neither of these rational policies implies the supposition of a conspiracy. The latter seems, unfortunately, a corollary of the crisis experience insofar as the catastrophic event at its focus "calls" for blaming a culprit. Right from the start of the COVID-19 pandemic, most media and politicians used extreme framings of the outbreak, including hyperbolic war metaphors and accusations against all kinds of "other" groups (Wodak 2021; Musolff 2022, 2024; Birchall & Knight 2023). The public were thus invited to search for conspiracy culprits to blame for either an apocalyptic attack on humanity or for its monstrous invention. A first counterstrategy for all responsible media has to be to separate the empathetic coverage of the human emotional impact of that crisis experience from a causal explanation of its trigger event and to defend the latter against attempts to reinterpret it in a conspiracist vein. This may be hard to achieve, but wildly speculating about potential conspiracies behind the crisis and disseminating them *ad infinitum* for the sake of sensationalist publications may come at the cost of having to spend much more time and effort in "debunking" them later. Hence, a "self-inoculation" against ventilating conspiracy fantasies and bogus statistics might be a good guidance for all media, but it is especially so for the "quality press," which likes to claim for itself an "enlightened" position vis-à-vis other media's supposedly more sensationalist–conspiracist leanings, only to disseminate hoax CTs further under the guise of "critical coverage." A second strategy has to be taking hoax CTs as seriously as other CTs by attacking the dissemination of their conspiracist speculation, for example by challenging vague allegations and exposing them as vacuous, rather than getting bogged down in details about inaccessible data.

Deconstructing the "Backstory" of CTs

Generally speaking, ascribing responsibility for a crisis or catastrophe to a group of conspirators is an epistemically viable *possible* explanation, and of course no media can afford not to report on it if a conspiracy story is already in circulation. However, it is one thing to report and comment on it with a view to exploring it further in detail and investigate its provenance, plausibility, and so on, and it is quite another thing to disseminate it and validate it simply on the grounds that is was propagated by a prominent official or "influential" public voice and has become a "trending" story. However, this is what happened in most of the media's treatments of the "lab-leak" origin story for COVID-19, where every utterance proposing it – whether by president X, scientist Y, or other "well-informed" sources – was treated as if it were already a confirmation of the lab-leak "fact" (and of the anti-Chinese CT derived from it). Such a repeated quoting practice can build up to a self-sustaining "argument from authority" by way of mutual endorsements which never question the reliability of the "authority" in question.

Another pseudo-argumentative strategy that is utilized in asserting CTs is a vague conclusion based on *cui bono* speculation. It derives its "proof" of a conspiracy's responsibility for a crisis or catastrophe from their perceived "beneficiary" status (e.g. financial gains of "Big Pharma" from COVID-19 and from the vaccination campaign). This argument, which also figures prominently in popular text types such as crime or detective stories, fairy tales, and soap operas, turns the CT into a "story with a lesson." It "leads" its recipients to a seemingly self-evident and emotionally involving conclusion that a few well-known "culprits" (e.g. Gates, Soros, Rothschild) and a larger circle of still hidden conspirators must be behind the crisis, and that only uncovering the "whole" cabal will put an end to their malevolent influence. Given the popular appeal of this type of story, public voices need to reflect self-critically on their role in framing a crisis or catastrophe in terms of a mystery story. Revealing mysteries is a key task (and key business) of investigative journalism but it also involves taking editorial responsibility by critically reviewing one's sources, including their political and/or economic interests in telling their story (Renner 2020). Any uncritical reiteration of speculative mystery narratives solely based on an unspecified *cui bono* argument must be exposed as unethical, and the excuse that it constitutes a mere exercise of the "right of free speech" as hypocritical.

Deconstructing the "Conclusion" That the Imminent Crisis or Catastrophe Proves the Conspiracy Backstory

The circular argument fallacy provides the frame for all CTs and also leads to the never-ending searches for "supporting" evidence of secret communications among the conspirators; for example, in the case of COVID-19, that China had traitor–insiders in the West, such as A. Fauci, who helped to cover up its guilt; for 9/11, that Jews were warned ahead of the attack not to go to work in the Twin Towers; for "Climategate," that internal debates among scientists proved their fabrication of the climate change hoax; for the Kennedy assassination and the 1972 Watergate break-in, that they were "false flag" operations of US secret services to incriminate other parties. The number of such CT-based speculations is indefinite and their (re-)invention is, as has been argued here, inevitable. Their "conclusions" are unfalsifiable due to their circularity. Hence, there is a danger for even the most critical and investigative media or independent (e.g. academic) institutions of getting side-tracked into researching the elusive evidence, thus inadvertently keeping the CT itself in play far beyond its sell-by date.

Ironically, when people conduct this search for further data in an open-ended way, they also make themselves vulnerable to being attacked as being part (or gullible victims) of the conspiracy. For if the "proof" of the CT is thought to lie self-evidently in the crisis or catastrophe, any doubting of the CT backstory and its "further" details can only be viewed as an irrational rejection of obvious facts, and the insistence on their critical investigation as a refusal to "see the larger picture" and "connect the dots" (Mason 2022). This predicament creates a true dilemma for CT critics because they cannot afford *not* to investigate the alleged "supporting evidence," whilst their research (and its public coverage) extends the very CT that they aim to debunk. It is therefore incumbent on CT critics to contextualize their own statements about investigating supposed new evidence in such a way that its conspiracist assumptions are exposed. In addition, they need to make explicit non-CT-based crisis explanations. These may be may well be less attractive stories than mystery scenarios and may necessitate sophisticated presentation techniques in order to have a realistic chance in the memetic contest of public crisis representations and interpretations. In the wake of the COVID-19 pandemic, some model initiatives in this direction have been developed, in the form of blogs, to explain the complex virological and epidemiological subject matter to the wider public and to specific target groups such as school children (Chen 2020; Hudgens 2020; Muelas-Gil 2022; National Institutes of Health 2024). In this way, the "reassuring" function of CTs can be neutralized and replaced by fact-based explanations that validate legitimate curiosity.

Deconstructing the "Resistance Fight" Solution of a CT Scenario

The cognitive and emotional "fulfilment" of all CTs lies in the public exposure and "proof" of the suspected conspiracy, which is likely to include a violent confrontation with the conspirators or their "henchmen." In such a confrontation, the CT propagators and believers enact the role of heroic *liberation* or *resistance fighters* who rescue the public from the impending or present crisis that was caused by the conspiracy. This fairy-tale ending is, however, often largely imaginary. The attempted "storming" of the German parliament building by Reich citizen protesters in August 2020 and the temporary occupation of the US Capitol in January 2021 by Trump supporters (who acted on a mix of COVID-19 hoax CTs, QAnon-myths, and "Stop the Steal" resentment) were both ended by the police and followed up by judicial persecutions, which were annulled for the Capitol storming by President Trump after his 2024 reelection. But as we saw in the testimonies of the German Reich citizens, even the thwarted action provided retrospectively passionate feelings of solidarity and collective self-confirmation.

This strong experience of in-group solidarity and a momentary resolution of cognitive dissonances about the world they live in motivates them to persevere in reproducing and reenacting their identity as "resistance fighters." There is ample historical and contemporary evidence of such experiences being exploited for attacking supposed "traitors" who supposedly aided and abetted of the alleged conspiracies long after their first "indictment" by the CT propagators, as exemplified by the concerted PR campaigns against Dreyfus supporters, the show-trial against the alleged communist conspiracy behind the Reichstag arson staged by the Nazis, the Stalinist show-trials of communists supposedly conspiring with capitalists, and the extended investigations of alleged "rogue scientists" in the Climategate and COVID-19 cases. The history of "CTs of long duration" such as those based on the *Protocols of the Elders of Zion*, anti-Free-Mason CTs, or witch CTs show that these follow-up campaigns have kept the core CTs alive and in play for centuries through adapting to new sociocultural environments and generating new "freedom fight" scenarios.

It is therefore crucially important to prevent the pseudo-confirmatory CT scenario enactments (as distinct from the ever-present CT opinions) and their revivals by critiquing them preemptively and prosecuting them judicially after they have happened. Typically, CT propagators will try to belittle and downplay their scenario enactments as not falling under civil or criminal law, as is, for instance, the case with Reich citizen defendants in German courts (*Frankfurter Allgemeine Zeitung* 2024a). That defense is, however, utterly hypocritical. In some cases it amounts to a rather transparent denial of having been present at or actively involved in violent "resistance" actions or their preparation (*Frankfurter Allgemeine Zeitung* 2024b, 2024c). In other apologetic moves, however, CT propagators go to astonishing lengths. Within the Reich citizen movement, some websites have started to denounce the German term "Reichsbürger" itself, once proudly adopted to signal alliance with the old German Empire, as a term of stigmatization invented by German state authorities to denounce the innocent free-thinking freedom fighter. The "grounds" for this defense is supposed to lie in definitions of "Reichsbürger" in the 1935 Nazi laws which excluded Jewish people from German citizenship (see website, *Beweisführung* 2025). The term is thus reinterpreted to be a "derogatory, stigmatizing Nazi word" that has been "taken over" by postwar Germany to prosecute *all* critics of the state, including, as it so happens, far-right extremists who otherwise hark back nostalgically to the 1871–1918 Empire or even to Nazi "Third Reich" (*Beweisführung* 2025).

This pseudo-argumentation turns the historical meaning of "Reichsbürger" on its head. For the Nazis, it was of course a term of highest praise and self-identification, not a stigma. Foreigners and enemies of the Reich were denied it. By rejecting that label for themselves, today's Reich citizens (who mostly support racist and xenophobic exclusion policies and deny the Holocaust) try to present themselves as anti-fascist heroes who are persecuted by the present-day continuation of the Nazi state and whose actions should therefore be accorded the same moral legitimacy as that of the historical anti-Nazi fighters (e.g. by fighting the police and trying to overthrow the state, as in 2020–2022).

As each fight scenario's enactment gives CT propagators and believers a momentary victory, inspiring them to spin the CT further (e.g. in post-2020 AfD propaganda [AfD 2020, 2022] or MAGA-inspired reinterpretations of the Capitol storming as a heroic victory [Van Dijcke & Wright 2021]), anti-CT campaigns must concentrate on preventing the enactment and revival of CT scenarios through obstructing their online meme-dissemination and apologetic reinterpretation, which has become the preferred *modus operandi* of conspiracy theorists today. This includes the robust denunciation of all CT-based speech acts that constitute incitement of violence and hate speech (Lee 2021, 2022; Kupper & Dittrich 2023) as criminal activities which are not protected by the right to free speech. Equally important is it for CT critics to admit that deconstructing CTs may involve the construction of "counter-CTs," insofar as a conspiracy may be suspected – rightly or wrongly – as being the origin of a CT. This seemingly paradoxical conclusion can be mitigated only by the CT critics' readiness to explain, question, and transparently correct their own counter-CTs when they are challenged in argumentation. Taking that risk is unavoidable and should not be a deterrent, for failing to acknowledge it would mean capitulation in fighting socially detrimental CTs. Historically, CT propagators who came to power and who managed to enact their "theories" have caused social and political mega-catastrophes. The philosopher (and early user of the term *conspiracy theory*), Karl Popper, named two such cases, Lenin and Hitler, as, respectively, believers in "Vulgar Marxist" and anti-Semitic CTs, which wreaked huge destruction but, as he asserts, eventually "failed to consummate their conspiracies" (Popper 1962: 125). However, the failure of their CTs came at the cost of tens of millions of victims and is not much of a consolation in view of the suffering which they caused. If we want to prevent socially catastrophic CTs from reaching the scenario stage of violent or even genocidal enactment, we need to deconstruct them before they become self-fulfilling prophecies.

References

AfD. (2020). Corona-Demo findet statt: Sieg der Freiheit!. *AfD Kompakt. Mitglieder-Magazin.*

AfD. (2022). Corona in Dauerschleife. Lauterbach braucht sein Virus. *AfD Kompakt. Mitglieder-Magazin.*

Allain, M. L., Bhattarai, A., McNeally, P., & Medina, R. M. (2023). Stopping the Steal: The Ecology of Conspiracy in a Politically Polarized Nation. *The Professional Geographer,* 76(1). 37–47.

Andone, C. & Lomelí Hernández, J. A. (2022). On Arguments from Ignorance in Policy-Making. In S. Oswald et al. (eds.). *The Pandemic of Argumentation*, 105–123. Cham: Springer.

Arendt, H. (1973). *The Origins of Totalitarianism.* New York: Harcourt Brace Jovanovich.

Aunger, R. (ed.). (2000). *Darwinizing Culture: The Status of Memetics as a Science.* Oxford: Oxford University Press.

Aupers, S. (2020). Decoding Mass Media/Decoding Conspiracy Theory. In M. Butter & P. Knight (eds.). *The Routledge Handbook of Conspiracy Theories,* 469–482. London/New York: Routledge.

Ayto, J. (2010). *Oxford Dictionary of English Idioms.* Oxford: Oxford University Press.

Baden, C. & Sharon, T. (2020). BLINDED BY THE LIES? Toward an Integrated Definition of Conspiracy Theories. *Communication Theory*, 31(1). 82–106.

Baier, B. & Re, G. (2020). Sources Believe Coronavirus Outbreak Originated in Wuhan Lab as Part of China's Efforts to Compete with US. *Fox News,* 15 April 2020.

Baker, P. & Glasser, S. (2022). *The Divider: Trump in the White House 2017–2021.* New York: Doubleday.

Banco, E. & Lippman, D. (2021). Top Trump Officials Pushed the Coronavirus "lab leak" Theory. Investigators Had Doubts. *Politico,* 16 June 2021.

Barkun, M. (2013). *A Culture of Conspiracy: Apocalyptic Visions in Contemporary America.* Berkeley: University of California Press.

Barkun, M. (2015). Conspiracy Theories as Stigmatized Knowledge. *Diogenes,* 62(3–4). 114–120.

Baudrillard, J. (1991). *La guerre du golfe n'a pas eu lieu.* Paris: Éditions galilée.

Begley, S. 2020. Trump Said More Covid19 Testing Creates More Cases. We Did the Math. *Statnews*, 20 July 2020. www.statnews.com/2020/07/20/trump-said-more-covid19-testing-creates-more-cases-we-did-the-math/.

Bein, A. (1965). Der jüdische Parasit. *Vierteljahreshefte für Zeitgeschichte*, 13. 121–149.

Benoit, W. L. (1997). Image repair discourse and crisis communication. *Public Relations Review*, 23(2). 177–186.

Berger, P. & Luckmann, T. (1991). *The Social Construction of Reality: A Treatise in the Sociology of Knowledge*. London: Penguin.

Bergmann, E. & Butter, M. (2020). Conspiracy Theory and Populism. In M. Butter & P. Knight (eds.), *The Routledge Handbook of Conspiracy Theories*, 330–343. London/New York: Routledge.

Bergmann, E. (2025). *The Weaponization of Conspiracy Theories*. London/New York: Routledge.

Beweisführung der politischen Verfolgung kritischer Menschen, Bevölkerungsteile und der echten Opposition in Deutschland mit der Reichsbürger Lüge, *VK.Com 2025*. https://vk.com/@whitewarti-beweisfuhrung-der-politischen-verfolgung-kritischer-menschen.

Birchall, C. & Knight, P. (2023). *Conspiracy Theories in the Time of Covid-19*. London/New York: Routledge.

Birchall, C. & Knight, P. (2024). Has Conspiracy Theory Run Out of Steam? In F. Beckman & J. de Leo (eds.). *Theory Conspiracy*, 149–167. London/New York: Routledge.

Blackmore, S. (1999). *The Meme Machine*. Foreword by Richard Dawkins. Oxford: Oxford University Press.

Blake, A. (2017). Kellyanne Conway Says Donald Trump's Team Has "alternative facts." Which Pretty Much Says It All. *The Washington Post*, 22 January 2017. www.washingtonpost.com/news/thefix/wp/2017/01/22/kellyanne-conway-says-donald-trumps-team-has-alternate-facts-which-pretty-much-says-it-all/.

Bloom, M. & Moskalenko, S. (2021). *Pastels and Pedophiles. Inside the Mind of QAnon*. Ithaca, NY: Stanford University Press.

Bok, S., Martin, D. E., & Lee, M. (2021). Validation of the COVID-19 Disbelief Scale: Conditional Indirect Effects of Religiosity and COVID-19 Fear on Intent to Vaccinate. *Acta Psychologica*, 219. 103382. https://doi.org/10.1016/j.actpsy.2021.103382.

Bondi, M. & Sanna, L. (2022). Exploring the Echo Chamber Concept: A Linguistic Perspective. In M. Demata, V. Zorzi & A. Zottola (eds.). *Conspiracy Theory Discourses*, 143–167. Amsterdam: John Benjamins.

Breitbart. (2021a). Top Scientist Claims Anthony Fauci "Untruthful" about Chinese Lab Research. *Breitbart*, 7 September 2021. www.breitbart.com/asia/2021/09/07/report-top-scientist-claims-anthony-fauci-untruthful-about-chinese-lab-research/.

Breitbart. (2021b). NIH Contradicts Fauci, Admits Funding Gain-of-Function Research at Wuhan Lab. *Breitbart*, 20 October 2021. www.breitbart.com/politics/2021/10/20/nih-contradicts-fauci-admits-funding-gain-of-function-research-at-wuhan-lab/.

Breitbart. (2023). Paul: We Know That First Days of the Pandemic Fauci "Orchestrated an Elaborate Cover-Up." *Breitbart*, 18 June 2023. www.breitbart.com/clips/2023/06/18/paul-we-know-that-first-days-of-the-pandemic-fauci-orchestrated-an-elaborate-cover-up/.

Brodie, R. (1996). *Virus of the Mind: The New Science of the Meme*. Seattle, WA: Integral Press.

Bronner, S. (2000). *A Rumor about the Jews: Reflections on Antisemitism and the Protocols of the Elders of Zion*. New York: St. Martin's Press.

Brooks, B. (2020). Like the Flu? Trump's Coronavirus Messaging Confuses Public, Pandemic Researchers Say. *Reuters*, 14 March 2020. www.reuters.com/article/us-health-coronavirus-mixed-messages-idUSKBN2102GY.

Brown, F. (2010). *For the Soul of France: Culture Wars in the Age of Dreyfus*. New York: A.A. Knopf.

Brugman, B. C. & Burgers, C. (2018). Political Framing across Disciplines: Evidence from 21st century Experiments. *Research & Politics*, 5(2). 1–7. https://doi.org/10.1177/2053168018783370.

Brumfiel, G. (2022). Their Mom Died of COVID. They Say Conspiracy Theories Are What Really Killed Her. *National Public Radio*, 24 April 2022. www.npr.org/sections/health-shots/2022/04/24/1089786147/covid-conspiracy-theories.

Bruns, A., Harrington, S., & Hurcombe, E. (2020). "Corona? 5G? or both?": The Dynamics of COVD-19/5G Conspiracy Theories on Facebook. *Media International Australia* 177(1). 12–29.

Buranyi, S. (2021). Why the "lab-leak" Theory of Covid's Origins has Gained Prominence again. *The Guardian*, 29 May 2021.

Butler, S. 2020. Conclusion Shopping. www.suebutler.com.au/new-words/2020/5/3/conclusion-shopping.

Butter, M. & Knight, P. (2020a). General Introduction. In M. Butter & P. Knight (eds.). *The Routledge Handbook of Conspiracy Theories*, 1–8. London/New York: Routledge.

Butter, M. & Knight, P. (2020b). Conspiracy Theory in Historical, Cultural and Literary Studies. In M. Butter and P. Knight (eds.). *The Routledge*

Handbook of Conspiracy Theories, 28–42. London/New York: Routledge.

Butter, M. & Knight, P. (2023). *Covid Conspiracy Theories in Global Perspective*. London/New York: Routledge.

Butter, M., Hatzikidi, K., Jeitler, C., Loperfido, G., & Turza, L. (eds.). (2024). *Populism and Conspiracy Theory: Case Studies and Theoretical Perspectives*. London/New York: Routledge.

Byford, J. (2011). *Conspiracy Theories: A Critical Introduction*. Basingstoke: Palgrave Macmillan.

Bytwerk, R. L. (2015). Believing in "Inner Truth": The Protocols of the Elders of Zion in Nazi Propaganda, 1933–1945. *Holocaust and Genocide Studies*, 29(2). 212–229.

Chen, T. (2020). The Pandemic Is Turning Some Doctors and Nurses into Social Media Stars. But Some Aren't Sure It's a Good Thing. *Buzzfeed News*, 18 April 2020. www.buzzfeednews.com/article/tanyachen/pandemic-turning-some-doctors-and-nurses-into-stars.

Chlup, R. (2023). Conspiracy Narratives as a Type of Social Myth. *International Journal of Politics, Culture, and Society*. https://doi.org/10.1007/s10767-023-09454-1.

CNN. (2020). Nation's Top Coronavirus Expert Dr. Anthony Fauci Forced to Beef up Security as Death Threats Increase. *CNN*, 2 April 2020.

Coady, D. (2018). An Introduction to the Philosophical Debate about Conspiracy Theories. In D. Coady (ed.). *Conspiracy Theories: The Philosophical Debate*, 1–12. London/New York: Routledge.

Cohn, N. (1967). *Warrant for Genocide: The Myth of the Jewish World Conspiracy and the Protocols of the Elders of Zion*. New York: Harper & Row.

Cohn, N. (1975). *Europe's Inner Demons: An Enquiry Inspired by the Great Witch-Hunt*. London: Chatto.

Cook, J., Lewandowsky, S., & Ecker, U. K. H. (2017). Neutralizing Misinformation through Inoculation: Exposing Misleading Argumentation Techniques Reduces Their Influence. *PloS One*, 12(5). e0175799. https://doi.org/10.1371/journal.pone.0175799.

Cook, N. & Choi, M. (2020). Trump Rallies His Base to Treat Coronavirus as a "hoax". *Politico*, 28 February 2020. www.politico.com/news/2020/02/28/trump-south-carolina-rally-coronavirus-118269.

Correctiv. (2024). *Der AfD-Komplex*. Essen: Correctiv.org.

Costello, T. H., Pennycook, G., & Rand, D. G. (2024). Durably Reducing Conspiracy Beliefs through Dialogues with AI. *Science*, 385. eadq1814. https://doi.org/10.1126/science.adq1814.

Coupland, N. (ed.). (2010). *The Handbook of Language and Globalization.* Oxford: Wiley-Blackwell.
Croft, W. (2000). *Explaining Language Change: An Evolutionary Approach.* London: Longman.
Croft, W. & Cruse, D. A. (2004). *Cognitive Linguistics.* Cambridge: Cambridge University Press.
Danesi, M. (2023). *Politics, Lies and Conspiracy Theories: A Cognitive Linguistic Perspective.* London/New York: Routledge.
Dawkins, R. (1976). *The Selfish Gene.* Oxford: Oxford University Press.
Dawkins, R. (1999). *The Extended Phenotype: The Long Reach of the Gene.* Oxford: Oxford University Press.
Dawkins, R. (2004). Viruses of the Mind. In Latha Menon (ed.). *A Devil's Chaplain. Selected Essays*, 151–172. London: Phoenix.
d'Ancona, M. (2017). *Post-Truth: The New War on Truth and How to Fight Back.* London: Ebury Press.
de Blécourt, W. (2013). Sabbath Stories Towards a New History of Witches' Assemblies. In B. P. Levack (ed.). *The Oxford Handbook of Witchcraft in Early Modern Europe and Colonial America*, 84–100. Oxford: Oxford University Press.
de Changy, F. (2021). *The Disappearing Act: The Impossible Case of MH370.* London: HarperCollins.
Demata, M., Zorzi, V., & Zottola, A. (eds.) (2022). *Conspiracy Theory Discourses.* Amsterdam: John Benjamins.
Der Spiegel. (2020). Chaostag, Chaosnacht. *Der Spiegel*, 7 November 2020.
Der Spiegel. (2022). Die Putschfantasien der »Reichsbürger«-Truppe. *Der Spiegel*, 9 December 2022.
Der Spiegel. (2023a). Mutmaßliche Terrorgruppe. *Der Spiegel*, 17 May 2023.
Der Spiegel. (2023b). Angeklagter soll mehr als 14 Jahre in Haft. *Der Spiegel,* 15 November 2023.
Der Tagesspiegel. (2020). Heilpraktikerin aus der Eifel: Das ist die Frau, die zum Sturm auf den Reichstag rief. *Der Tagesspiegel,* 1 September 2020.
Deschrijver, C. (2021). On the Metapragmatics of "conspiracy theory": Scepticism and Epistemological Debates in Online Conspiracy Comments. *Journal of Pragmatics*, 182. 310–321.
Deutsche Welle. (2008). Legal Ruling. *Deutsche Welle,* 01//11/2008. www.dw.com/en/court-overturns-nazi-verdict-on-reichstag-arsonist/a-3052896.
Deutsche Welle. (2020). Corona-Ermächtigungsgesetz? Warum der Vergleich mit 1933 täuscht. 18 November 2020.

Deutsche Welle. (2022). "Reichsbürger": Ist ein Umsturz denkbar? *Deutsche Welle,* 8 December 2022.

Die Welt. (2020a). Die gefährliche Legende vom "Sturm". *Die Welt,* 30 August 2020.

Die Welt. (2020b). Besetzte Reichstagstreppe – Was kurz davor tatsächlich geschah. *Die Welt,* 31 August 2020.

Die Welt. (2022). Reichsbürger»-Ideologie und Verschwörungsmythen. *Die Welt,* 7 December 2022.

Die Welt. (2023). Was wollen «Reichsbürger»? Und wie gefährlich sind sie?. *Die Welt,* 22 March 2023.

Die Zeit. (2020). Sie brauchten nur dieses eine Foto. *Die Zeit,* 31 August 2020.

Die Zeit. (2023). Warum haben Sie mitgemacht? *Die Zeit,* 24 August 2023.

Douglas, K. M., Uscinski, J. E., Sutton, R. S., Chichocka, A., Nefes, T., Ang, S. A., & Deravi, F. (2019). Understanding Conspiracy Theories. *Advances in Political Psychology,* 40(Suppl. 1). 3–35. https://doi.org/10.1111/pops.12568.

Douglas, M. (1970). *Natural Symbols. Explorations in Cosmology.* London: Routledge.

Dunbar, D. & Reagan, B. (eds.). (2011). *Debunking 9/11 Myths: Why Conspiracy Theories Can't Stand up to the Facts: An In-depth Investigation by Popular Mechanics.* New York: Hearst Communications.

Dundes, A. (1991). *The Blood Libel Legend: A Casebook in Anti-Semitic Folklore.* Madison: The University of Wisconsin Press.

Dyrendal, A., Kennair, L. E. O., & Bendixen, M. (2021). Predictors of Belief in Conspiracy Theory: The Role of Individual Differences in Schizotypal Traits, Paranormal Beliefs, Social Dominance Orientation, Right Wing Authoritarianism and Conspiracy Mentality. *Personality and Individual Differences,* 173(2021). 110645. https://doi.org/10.1016/j.paid.2021.110645.

Elmer, P. (2013a). Science and Witchcraft. In B. P. Levack (ed.). *The Oxford Handbook of Witchcraft in Early Modern Europe and Colonial America,* 548–560. Oxford: Oxford University Press.

Elmer, P. (2013b). Medicine and Witchcraft. In B. P. Levack (ed.). *The Oxford Handbook of Witchcraft in Early Modern Europe and Colonial America,* 561–574. Oxford: Oxford University Press.

Emmery, R. (2022). "Een samenzwering van kwaadaardige reptielen": ophef in Nederland over uitspraken van politicus en complotdenker Thierry Baudet, *vrt nws,* 18 October 2022. www.vrt.be/vrtnws/nl/2022/10/17/baudet-reptielen/.

Entman, R. M. (1993). Framing: Toward Clarification of a Fractured Paradigm. *Journal of Communication*, 43(4). 51–58. https://doi.org/10.1111/j.1460-2466.1993.tb01304.x.

Evanega, S., Lynas, M., Adams, J., & Smolenjak, K. (2020). *Coronavirus Misinformation: Quantifying Sources and Themes in the COVID-19 "infodemic"*. Ithaca, NY: Cornell University. https://allianceforscience.cornell.edu/wp-content/uploads/2020/10/Evanega-et-al-Coronavirus-misinformation-submitted072320-1.pdf.

Evans, R. J. (2005). *The Third Reich in Power, 1933–1939*. London: Penguin.

Evans, R. J. (2020). *The Hitler Conspiracies: The Third Reich and the Paranoid Imagination*. London: Penguin.

Evans-Pritchard, E. E. (1950). *Witchcraft, Oracles and Magic among the Azande*. Oxford: Clarendon Press.

Fauconnier, G. & Turner, M. (2002). *The Way We Think: Conceptual Blending and the Mind's Hidden Complexities*. New York: Basic Books.

Fichtelberg, A. (2006). Conspiracy and International Criminal Justice. *Criminal Law Forum* 17(2). https://doi.org/10.1007/s10609-006-9013-6.

Fillmore, Charles J. (1985). Frames and the Semantics of Understanding. *Quaderni di Semantica,* 6(2). 222–253.

Forberg, P. L. (2021). From the Fringe to The Fore: An Algorithmic Ethnography of the Far-Right Conspiracy Theory Group QAnon. *Journal of Contemporary Ethnography*. https://doi.org/10.1177/08912416211040560.

Frankfurter Allgemeine Zeitung. (2024a). Nie geplant, den Bundestag zu stürmen. *Frankfurter Allgemeine Zeitung*, 4 April 2024.

Frankfurter Allgemeine Zeitung. (2024b). Angeklagter Reichsbürger bestätigt Erkundung im Bundestag. *Frankfurter Allgemeine Zeitung*, 13 August 2024.

Frankfurter Allgemeine Zeitung. (2024c). Haftstrafe nach rechten Umsturzplänen. 14 August 2024.

Gagné, M. J. (2022). *Thinking Critically about the Kennedy Assassination: Debunking the Myths and Conspiracy Theories*. London/New York: Routledge.

Gallagher, J. (2024). Genetic Ghosts Suggest Covid's Market Origins. *BBC*, 10/09/2014. www.bbc.com/news/articles/cy8095xjg4po.

Garcés-Conejos Blitvich, P. & Lorenzo-Dus, N. (2022). "Go ahead and 'debunk' Truth by Calling It a Conspiracy Theory." The Discursive Construction of Conspiracy Theoryness in Online Affinity Spaces.

In M. Demata, V. Zorzi & A. Zottola (eds.). *Conspiracy Theory Discourses*, 71–98. Amsterdam: John Benjamins.

Garwood, C. (2007). *Flat Earth: The History of an Infamous Idea*. New York: St. Martin's Press.

Girard, P. (2020). Conspiracy Theories in Europe during the Twentieth Century. In M. Butter & P. Knight (eds.). *The Routledge Handbook of Conspiracy Theories,* 569–581. London/New York: Routledge.

Gladchuk, J. J. (2006). *Hollywood and Anticommunism: HUAC and the Evolution of the Red Menace, 1935–1950*. London/New York: Routledge.

Goebbels, J. (1993). *Die Tagebücher von Joseph Goebbels*. Ed. E. Fröhlich. Munich: K. G. Saur.

Golec de Zavala, A., Bierwiaczonek, K., & Ciesielski, P. (2022). An Interpretation of Meta-analytical Evidence for the Link between Collective Narcissism and Conspiracy Theories. *Current Opinion in Psychology*, 47. 101360. https://doi.org/10.1016/j.copsyc.2022.101360.

Guttenplan, D. D. (2001). *The Holocaust on Trial: History, Justice and the David Irving Libel Case*. London: Granta.

Habermas, J. (1972). Vorbereitende Bemerkungen zu einer Theorie der kommunikativen Kompetenz. In H. Holzer & K. Steinbacher (eds.). *Sprache und Gesellschaft*, 208–236. Hamburg: Hoffmann & Campe.

Hagemeister, M. (2022). *The Perennial Conspiracy Theory: Reflections on the History of the Protocols of the Elders of Zion*. London/New York: Routledge.

Hall Jamieson, K. (2021). How Conspiracists Exploited COVID-19 Science. *Nature Human Behaviour* 5 (1 November 2021). 1464–1465.

Hall Jamieson, K., Levendusky, M., & Pasek, J. (2023). "Stop the Steal": The Rhetoric of Electoral Delegitimacy. In K. Hall Jamieson, M. Levendusky, J. Pasek, R. L. Holbert, A. Renninger, Y. Ophir, D. Walter, B. Hardy, K. Kenski, K. Winneg & D. Romer (eds.). *Democracy Amid Crises: Polarization, Pandemic, Protests, and Persuasion*, 281–300. Oxford: Oxford University Press.

Herf, J. (2006). *The Jewish Enemy: Nazi Propaganda during World War II and the Holocaust*. Cambridge, MA: Belknap Press.

Hess, B.-J. (2000). *Seuchengesetzgebung in den Deutschen Staaten und im Kaiserreich vom ausgehenden 18. Jahrhundert bis zum Reichsseuchengesetz 1900*. Heidelberg: PhD University of Heidelberg.

Hitler, A. [1925/1927] (2016). *Mein Kampf – Eine Kritische Edition*. Eds. C. Hartmann, T. Vordermayer, O. Plöckinger & R. Töppel. Munich-Berlin: Institut für Zeitgeschichte.

Hitler, A. [1939] (1965). Rede vor dem Reichstag, 30. Januar 1939. In M. Domarus (ed.). *Hitler. Reden und Proklamationen 1932–1945. Kommentiert von einem deutschen Zeitgenossen*, vol. II/I, 1047–1061. Munich: Süddeutscher Verlag.

Hoffman, B. (2023). Understanding Hamas's Genocidal Ideology. *The Atlantic*, 10 October 2023. www.theatlantic.com/international/archive/2023/10/hamas-covenant-israel-attack-war-genocide/675602/.

Hofhuis, S. (2022). Qualitative Darwinism: An Evolutionary History of Witch-hunting. PhD. Utrecht: Utrecht University.

Hofhuis, S. & Boudry, M. (2019). "Viral" Hunts? A Cultural Darwinian Analysis of Witch Persecutions. *Cultural Science Journal*, 11(1). 13–29. https://doi.org/10.5334/csci.116.

Hofstadter, R. (1964). The Paranoid Style in American Politics. *Harper's Magazine*, November 1964. 77–86.

Hoft, J. (2021). Smoking Gun: Fauci Lied, Millions Died – Fauci Was Informed of Hydroxychloroquine Success in early 2020 but Lied to Public Instead Despite the Science #*FauciEmails*. *Gateway Pundit* (3 June 2021). https://archive.is/kgwEx#selection-612.0–612.1.

Holland, J. & Jarvis, L. (2024). COVID-19 and the Limits of Critical Security Theory: Securitization, Cosmopolitanism, and Pandemic Politics. *Journal of Global Security Studies*, 9(4). ogae031. https://doi.org/10.1093/jogss/ogae031.

Holoyda, B. J. (2022). The QAnon Conspiracy Theory and the Assessment of Its Believers. *The Journal of the American Academy of Psychiatry and the Law*, 50(1). 124–135.

Hotez, P. J. (2021a). COVID Vaccines: Time to Confront Anti-vax Aggression. *Nature*, 29/04/2021. https://doi.org/10.1038/d41586-021-01084-x.

Hotez, P. J. (2021b). Anti-science Kills: From Soviet Embrace of Pseudoscience to Accelerated Attacks on US Biomedicine. *PLoS Biology*, 19(1). e3001068. https://doi.org/10.1371/journal.pbio.3001068.

Hotez, P. J. (2023). *The Deadly Rise of Anti-Science: A Scientist's Warning*. Baltimore: Johns Hopkins University Press.

Hudgens, L. H. (2020). A Middle School Teacher's Creative Way of Framing the Pandemic for Children. *The Washington Post,* 20 April 2020.

Hyman, P. E. (2005). New Perspectives on the Dreyfus Affair. *Historical Reflections/Réflexions Historiques*, 31(3). 335–349.

Icke, D. (1999). *The Biggest Secret: The Book That Will Change the World*. Ilford: Bridge of Love Publications.

Imhoff, R. & Lamberty, P. (2020). A Bioweapon or a Hoax? The Link between Distinct Conspiracy Beliefs about the Coronavirus Disease (COVID-19) Outbreak and Pandemic Behavior. *Social Psychological and Personality Science*, 11(8). 1110–1118.

Imhoff, R., Bertlich, T., & Frenken, M. (2022). Tearing Apart the "evil" Twins: A General Conspiracy Mentality Is Not the Same as Specific Conspiracy Beliefs. *Current Opinion in Psychology* 47.101349. https://doi.org/10.1016/j.copsyc.2022.101349.

Inwood, O. & Zappavigna, M. (2022). The ID2020 Conspiracy Theory in YouTube Video Comments during COVID-19: Bonding around Religious, Political, and Technological Discourses. In M. Demata, V. Zorzi & A. Zottola (eds.). *Conspiracy Theory Discourses*, 241–266. Amsterdam: John Benjamins.

Israeli, R. (2017). *Blood Libel and Its Derivatives: The Scourge of Anti-Semitism*. London/New York: Routledge.

Jarvis, L. (2022). Counting Coronavirus: Mathematical Language in the UK Response to Covid-19. In A. Musolff, R. Breeze, K. Kondo & S. Vilar-Lluch (eds.). *Pandemic and Crisis Discourse: Communicating Covid-19 and Public Health Strategy*, 79–93. London: Bloomsbury.

Jennings, W., Stoker, G., Bunting, H., Valgarðsson, V. O., Gaskell, J., Devine, D., McKay, L., & Mills, M. C. (2021). Lack of Trust, Conspiracy Beliefs, and Social Media Use Predict COVID-19 Vaccine Hesitancy. *Vaccines*, 9. 593. https://doi.org/10.3390/vaccines9060593.

Jolley, D., Mari, S., & Douglas, K. M. (2020). Consequences of Conspiracy Theories. In M. Butter & P. Knight, *Routledge Handbook of Conspiracy Theories*, 231–241. London/New York: Routledge.

Kakisina, P. A., Indhiarti, T. R., & Al Fajri, M. S. (2022). Discursive Strategies of Manipulation in COVID-19 Political Discourse: The Case of Donald Trump and Jair Bolsonaro. *SAGE Open, January–March 2022*: 1–9. https://doi.org/10.1177/21582440221079884.

Kale, S. (2021). The Life and Tragic Death of John Eyers – A Fitness Fanatic Who Refused the Vaccine. *The Guardian*, 30 November 2021.

Kampf, Z. (2009). Public Non-apologies: The Discourse of Minimizing Responsibility. *Journal of Pragmatics*, 41(11). 2257–2270.

Keeley, B. L. (2018). Of Conspiracy Theories. In D. Coady (ed.). *Conspiracy Theories: The Philosophical Debate*, 45–60. London/New York: Routledge.

Keith, M. (2022). QAnon Influencer Who Spread Conspiracy Theories and Misinformation about COVID-19 Dies after Contracting the Virus. *Business Insider*, 8 January 2022.

Kennedy, R. F. Jr. (2021). *The Real Anthony Fauci: Bill Gates, Big Pharma and the Global War on Democracy and Public Health*. New York: Skyhorse Publishing.

Kennedy, R. F. Jr. (2023). *The Wuhan Cover-Up and the Terrifying Bioweapons Arms Race*. New York: Skyhorse Publishing.

Kessler, G. (2021). Fact-checking the Paul-Fauci Flap over Wuhan Lab Funding. *The Washington Post*. 18 May 2021.

King, R. H. (2017). The Law and the Holocaust. *Patterns of Prejudice*, 51(5). 439–452.

Kitta, A. (2012). *Vaccinations and Public Concern in History: Legend, Rumor, and Risk Perception*. London/New York: Routledge.

Knight, P. (2007). *The Kennedy Assassination*. Jackson: University Press of Mississippi.

Koley, T. K. & Dhole, M. (2021). *The COVID-19 Pandemic: The Deadly Coronavirus Outbreak*. London/New York: Routledge.

Korthals Altes, L. (2008). Irony. In D. Herman, M. Jahn & M.-L. Ryan (eds.). *Routledge Encyclopedia of Narrative Theory*, 261–263. London/New York: Routledge.

Kozlov, M. (2023). US COVID Origins Hearing Produces Heat But No Light on COVID-origins Debate. Nature, 20 July 2023.

Kozlov, M. (2024). US Hearing Produces Puts Scientific Journals in the Hot Seat. Nature, 16 April 2024.

Krammer, F. (2020). SARS-CoV-2 Vaccines in Development. *Nature*, 586(7830). 516–527. https://doi.org/10.1038%2Fs41586-020-2798-3.

Krekó, P. (2020). Countering Conspiracy Theories and Misinformation. In M. Butter & P. Knight (eds.). *The Routledge Handbook of Conspiracy Theories*, 242–255. London/New York: Routledge.

Krumeich, G. (1989). Einkreisung. Zur Entstehung und Bedeutung eines politischen Schlagwortes. *Sprache und Literatur in Wissenschaft und Unterricht*, 63. 99–104.

Krumeich, G. (2019). *Die unbewältigte Niederlage: Das Trauma des Ersten Weltkriegs und die Weimarer Republik*. Freiburg: Herder.

Kupper, J. & Dittrich, M. (2023). The Reichsbürger Coup: How the German COVID-19 Denier Scene and Anti-Lockdown Movement Became a Breeding Ground for Terrorism. *GNET*, 18 January 2023. https://gnet-research.org/2023/01/18/the-reichsburger-coup-how-the-german-covid-19-denier-scene-and-anti-lockdown-movement-became-a-breeding-ground-for-terrorism/.

Lakoff, G. (1987). *Women, Fire, and Dangerous Things: What Categories Reveal about the Mind.* Chicago: The University of Chicago Press.

Lakoff, G. (1993). The Contemporary Theory of Metaphor. In A. Ortony (ed.). *Metaphor and Thought,* 202–251. Cambridge: Cambridge University Press.

Lakoff, G. & Johnson, M. (1980). *Metaphors We Live By.* Chicago: The University of Chicago Press.

Lakoff, G. & Wehling, E. (2016). *Your Brain's Politics. How the Science of Mind Explains the Political Divide.* Exeter: Imprint Academic.

Landes, R. & Katz, S. T. (eds.) (2011). *The Paranoid Apocalypse. A Hundred-Year Retrospective on The Protocols of the Elders of Zion.* New York: New York University Press.

Langer, A. (2021). The Eternal George Soros: The Rise of Antisemitic and Islamophobic Conspiracy Theory. In A. Önnerfors & A. Krouwel (eds.). *Europe: Continent of Conspiracies: Conspiracy Theories in and about Europe,* 152–184. London/New York: Routledge.

Lantian, A., Wood, M., & Gjoneska, B. (2020). Personality Traits, Cognitive Styles, and Worldviews associated with Beliefs in Conspiracy Theories. In M. Butter & P. Knight (eds.). *The Routledge Handbook of Conspiracy Theories,* 155–167. London/New York: Routledge.

Ledford, H. (2021a). How Could a COVID Vaccine Cause Blood Clots? Scientists Race to Investigate. *Nature,* 9 April 2021. https://doi.org/10.1038/d41586-021-00940-0.

Ledford, H. (2021b). Should Children Get COVID Vaccines? What the Science Says. *Nature,* 20 July 2021. https://doi.org/10.1038/d41586-021-01898-9.

Lee, C. (2021). #HateIsAVirus: Talking about COVID-19 "Hate". In R. Jones (ed.). *Viral Discourse,* 61–68. Cambridge: Cambridge University Press.

Lee, C. (2022). COVID-19 Conspiracy Theories and Affective Discourse. In M. Demata, V. Zorzi & A. Zottola (eds.). *Conspiracy Theory Discourses,* 216–237. Amsterdam: John Benjamins.

Lee, E. W. J., Bao, H., Wang, Y., & Lim, Y. T. (2023). From Pandemic to Plandemic: Examining the Amplification and Attenuation of COVID-19 Misinformation on Social Media. *Social Science and Medicine,* 328.115979. https://doi.org/10.1016/j.socscimed.2023.115979.

Lehmann, H. & Ulbricht, O. (1992). Motive und Argumente von Gegnern der Hexenverfolgung von Weyer bis Spee. In H. Lehmann

& O. Ulbricht (eds.). *Vom Unfug des Hexen-Processes: Gegner der Hexenverfolgung von Johann Weyer bis Friedrich Spee*, 1–14. Wiesbaden: Harrassowitz.

Levack, B. (2006). *The Witch Hunt in Early Modern Europe*. London: Longman.

Levack, B. (ed.) (2013a). *The Oxford Handbook of Witchcraft in Early Modern Europe and Colonial America*. Oxford: Oxford University Press.

Levack, Brian P. (2013b). The Decline and End of Witchcraft Prosecutions. In *The Oxford Handbook of Witchcraft in Early Modern Europe and Colonial America,* 429–446. Oxford University Press.

Levy, N. (2024). Believing in Stories: Delusions, Superstitions, Conspiracy Theories, and Other Fairy Tales. In E. Sullivan-Bissett (ed.). *Belief, Imagination, and Delusion,* 129–146. Oxford: Oxford University Press.

Lewandowsky, S., Oberauer, K., & Gignac, G. E. (2013). NASA Faked the Moon Landing – Therefore, (climate) Science Is a Hoax: An Anatomy of the Motivated Rejection of Science. *Psychological Science,* 24(5). 622–633.

Lewiński, M. & Abreu, P. (2022). Arguing about "COVID": Metalinguistic Arguments on What Counts as a "COVID-19 Death". In S. Oswald, M. Lewiński, S. Greco & S. Villata (eds.). *The Pandemic of Argumentation,* 17–41. Cham: Springer.

Li, Y. D., Chi, W. Y., Su, J. H., Ferrall, L., Hung, C. F., & Wu, T. C. (2020). Coronavirus Vaccine Development: From SARS and MERS to COVID-19. *Journal of Biomedical Science.* 27(1). 104. https://doi.org/10.1186%2Fs12929-020-00695-2.

Ling, J. (2022). False Claims of U.S. Biowarfare Labs in Ukraine Grip QAnon. *Foreign Policy* blog, 2 March 2022. https://foreignpolicy.com/2022/03/02/ukraine-biolabs-conspiracy-theory-qanon/.

Lipstadt, D. (2017). *Denial: Holocaust History on Trial.* New York: Ecco.

Loh, M. (2022). How Russia's Invasion of Ukraine, Vampire Obsession, and "secret bio-weapons" Have Played into China's Narrative about COVID-19's Origin. *Business Insider,* 11 March 2022.

Lusher, A. (2016). Turkey Coup: Conspiracy Theorists Claim Power Grab Attempt Was Faked by Erdogan. *The Independent*, 17 July 2016.

Maci, S., Demata, M., McGlashan, M., & Seargeant, P. (eds.). (2024). *The Routledge Handbook of Discourse and Disinformation*. London/New York: Routledge.

Mahl, D., Schäfer, M. S., & Zeng, J. (2022). Conspiracy Theories in Online Environments: An Interdisciplinary Literature Review and Agenda for Future Research. *New Media & Society*, 24. 1781–1801.

Mallapaty, S. (2023). COVID Origins Study Links Racoon Dogs to Wuhan Market: What Scientists Think. *Nature,* 21 March 2023. https://doi.org/10.1038/d41586-023-00827-2.

Marinthe, G., Brown, G., Delouvée, S., & Jolley, D. (2020). Looking Out for Myself: Exploring the Relationship between Conspiracy Mentality, Perceived Personal Risk, and COVID-19 Prevention Measures. *British Journal of Health Psychology*, 25. 957–980. https://doi.org/10.1111/bjhp.12449.

Marshal, M. (2023). Long COVID: Answers Emerge on How Many People Get Better. *Nature,* 27 June 2023. https://doi.org/10.1038/d41586-023-02121-7.

Mason, J. (2022). "If you can't see the pattern here, there's something wrong": A Cognitive Account of Conspiracy Narratives, Schemas, and the Construction of the "expert". In M. Demata, V. Zorzi, & A. Zottola (eds.). *Conspiracy Theory Discourses,* 169–191. Amsterdam: John Benjamins.

Maxmen, A. & Mallapaty, S. (2021). The COVID Lab-leak Hypothesis: What Scientists Do and Don't Know. *Nature*, 594. 313–315 (8 June 2021). https://doi.org/10.1038/d41586-021-01529-3.

Mettraux, G. (ed.) 2008. *Perspectives on the Nuremberg Trial.* Oxford: Oxford University Press.

Meyssan, T. (2002). *9/11. The Big Lie.* London: Carnot Editions.

Miller, M. E. (2021). The Gunman Who Terrorized a D.C. Pizzeria Is out of Prison. The QAnon Conspiracy Theories He Helped Unleash Are Out of Control. *The Washington Post*, 16 February 2021.

Modern Healthcare. (2021). Nurses Fight Conspiracy Theories along with Coronavirus. *Modern Healthcare*, 13 March 2021. www.modernhealthcare.com/providers/nurses-fight-conspiracy-theories-along-coronavirus.

Muelas-Gil, M. (2022). Covid Warriors: An Analysis of the Use of Metaphors in Children's Books to Help Them Understand Covid-19. In A. Musolff, R. Breeze, K. Kondo & S. Vilar-Lluch (eds.). *Pandemic and Crisis Discourse. Communicating Covid-19 and Public Health Strategy*, 115–133. London: Bloomsbury.

Musolff, A. (2010). *Metaphor, Nation and the Holocaust: The Concept of the Body Politic.* London/New York: Routledge.

Musolff, A. (2016). *Political Metaphor Analysis: Discourse and Scenarios.* London: Bloomsbury.

Musolff, A. (2022). Fake-conspiracy: Trump's Anti-Chinese "COVID-19-as-war" Scenario. In M. Demata, V. Zorzi & A. Zottola (eds.). *Conspiracy Theory Discourses*, 121–139. Amsterdam: John Benjamins.

Musolff, A. (2024). War Metaphors and Conspiracy Theories. In M. Romano (ed.) *Metaphor in Social-political Contexts: Critical, Socio-Cognitive Approaches,* 159–176. Berlin/Boston: W. de Gruyter.

National Academies of Sciences, Engineering, and Medicine (ed.). (2023). *Attacks on Scientists and Health Professionals During the Pandemic. Proceedings of a Symposium – in Brief.* The National Academies Press. https://doi.org/10.17226/26936.

National Geographic. (2021). *Fauci: Expect the Unexpected: Ten Lessons on Truth, Service, and the Way Forward.* Washington, DC: National Geographic.

National Institutes of Health (NIH). 2024. *NIH Director's Blog.* https://directorsblog.nih.gov/tag/covid-19/.

Nelson, R. (2013). Sandy Hook Hero Harassed by Burgeoning Truther-movement. *Time,* 16 January 2013. https://newsfeed.time.com/2013/01/16/sandy-hook-hero-harassed-by-burgeoning-truther-movement/.

Newsweek. (2021). Pastor Says Fauci Should Be Waterboarded Until He Admits to Working with China to Create COVID. *Newsweek,* 4 December 2021.

Newsweek. (2023). Fauci Says He's Always Been "Honest" as COVID Origins Questions Raised. *Newsweek,* 8 March 2023.

NIAID (National Institute of Allergy and Infectious Diseases). (2023). Dr. Anthony Fauci, M.D. www.niaid.nih.gov/about/anthony-s-fauci-md-bio (accessed 12 May 2024).

Nichols, T. (2017). *The Death of Expertise: The Campaign against Established Knowledge and Why it Matters.* Oxford: Oxford University Press.

Nogrady, B. (2021). Scientists under Attack. *Nature,* 598. 250–253. https://doi.org/10.1038/d41586-021-02741-x.

Nogrady, B. (2024). Harassment of Scientists Is Surging. *Nature,* 629 (23 May 2024). 748–750. https://doi.org/10.1038/d41586-024-01468-9.

Norris, C. (1992). *Uncritical Theory: Postmodernism, Intellectuals and the Gulf War.* London: Lawrence & Wishart.

NPR/IPSOS. (2020). More than 1 in 3 Americans believe a "Deep State" Is Working to Undermine Trump: NPR/Ipsos Poll Finds Widespread Concerns about the Spread of False Information, Despite Some

Believing in COVID-19 and QAnon-related Conspiracies. *IPSOS Public Poll Findings and Methodology*, 30 December 2020. www.ipsos.com/sites/default/files/ct/news/documents/2020-12/topline_npr_misinformation_poll_123020.pdf.

Oberhauser, K. (2020). Freemasons, Illuminati and Jews: Conspiracy theories and the French Revolution. In M. Butter & P. Knight (eds.), *The Routledge Handbook of Conspiracy Theories*, 555–568. London/New York: Routledge.

Office of the United States Chief of Counsel for the Prosecution of Axis Criminality. (1946). *Nazi Conspiracy and Aggression*. Washington, DC: US Government.

Ohlheiser, A. W. (2020). Facebook and YouTube Are Rushing to Delete "Plandemic," a Conspiracy-laden Video. *MIT Technology Review*, 07 May 2020. www.technologyreview.com/2020/05/07/1001469/facebook-youtube-plandemic-covid-misinformation/.

Olmstead, M. (2022). The Fauci boogeyman. *Slate*, 16 February 2022.

Olmsted, E. (2023). Elon Musk Invites Alex Jones to Explain That "Whole Sandy Hook Thing". *The New Republic*, 11 December 2023. https://newrepublic.com/post/177455/alex-jones-says-just-playing-devils-advocate-whole-sandy-hook-thing.

Önnerfors, A. (2021). Der Grosse Austausch. Conspiratorial Frames of Terrorist Violence in Germany. In A. Önnerfors & Krouwel (eds.), *Europe: Continent of Conspiracies: Conspiracy Theories in and about Europe*, 62–70. London/New York: Routledge.

Otten, T. (2022). Infowars' Alex Jones Files for Bankruptcy After Sandy Hook Verdict. *The New Republic*, 2 December 2022. https://newrepublic.com/post/169275/infowars-alex-jones-files-bankruptcy-sandy-hook-verdict.

Pantenburg, J., Reichardt, S., & Sepp, B. (2021). Corona-Proteste und das (Gegen-) Wissen sozialer Bewegungen. *Aus Politik und Zeitgeschichte*, 15 January 2021. www.bpb.de/shop/zeitschriften/apuz/wissen-2021/325605/corona-proteste-und-das-gegen-wissen-sozialer-bewegungen/.

Pascovich, E. (2018). The Devil's Advocate in Intelligence: The Israeli Experience. *Intelligence and National Security*, 33(6). 854–865, https://doi.org/10.1080/02684527.2018.1470062.

Paul, R. (2023). *Deception. The Great Covid Cover-Up*. New York: Skyhorse Publishing.

Paun, C. (2023). Trump's CDC Director Says Fauci Shut Down Debate on Covid's Origin. *Politico*, 8 March 2023.

Pawelz, J. (2022). *Umsturzpläne und Verschwörungsdenken von "Reichsbürgern" und "Selbstverwaltern"*. Hamburg: Institut für

Friedensforschung und Sicherheitspolitik. https://ifsh.de/news-detail/umsturzplaene-und-verschwoerungsdenken-von-reichsbuergern-und-selbstverwaltern.

Pearce, F. (2010). *The Climate Files: The Battle for the Truth about Global Warming.* London: Guardian Books.

Pentucci, R. (2022). Extreme Right-Wing Terrorism and COVID-19 – A Two-Year Stocktake. *Counter-Terrorist Trends and Analyses*, 14 (3). 17–23.

Pertwee, E., Simas, C., & Larson, H. J. (2022). An Epidemic of Uncertainty: Rumors, Conspiracy Theories and Vaccine Hesitancy. *Nature Medicine Perspective.* 28 March 2022, 456–459. https://doi.org/10.1038/s41591-022-01728-z.

Petersen, K. (2022). Fact Check: Video Shows Rep. *Jim Jordan question Dr. Anthony Fauci. USA Today*, 14 November 2022.

Pigden, C. (2018). Popper revisited, or What Is Wrong with Conspiracy Theories? In D. Coady (ed.). *Conspiracy Theories. The Philosophical Debate,* 17–43. London/New York: Routledge.

Plümper, T., Neumayer, E., & Pfaff, K. G. (2021). The Strategy of Protest against Covid-19 Containment Policies in Germany. *Social Science Quarterly*, 102. 2236–2250. https://doi.org/10.1111/ssqu.13066.

Popper, K. R. (1962). *Conjectures and Refutations.* London: Routledge & Kegan Paul.

Powell, J. L. (2011). *The Inquisition of Climate Science.* New York: Columbia University Press.

Priemel, K. C. (2016). *The Betrayal: The Nuremberg Trials and German Divergence.* Oxford: Oxford University Press.

Putnam, H. (1975). The Meaning of "Meaning". In K. Gunderson (ed.). *Language, Mind and Knowledge*, 131–193. Minneapolis: University of Minnesota Press.

Rabo, A. (2020). Conspiracy Theory as Occult Cosmology in Anthropology. In M. Butter & P. Knight (eds.). *The Routledge Handbook of Conspiracy Theories,* 81–93. London/New York: Routledge.

Räikä, J. & Ritola, J. (2020). Philosophy and Conspiracy Theories. In M. Butter & P. Knight (eds.). *The Routledge Handbook of Conspiracy Theories*, 56–66. London/New York: Routledge.

Rajewsky, I. (2020). Theories of Fictionality and their Real Other. In M. Fludernik & M.-L. Ryan (eds.). *Narrative Factuality. A Handbook,* 29–50. Berlin/New York: De Gruyter.

Rathje, J. (2017). *"Reichsbürger" – Verschwörungsideologie mit deutscher Spezifik. Wissen schafft Demokratie – Schriftenreihe des Instituts für Demokratie und Zivilgesellschaft (IDZ)*, 1. 238–249.

Rathje, J. (2021). "Reichsbürger" und Souveränismus. *Aus Politik und Zeitgeschichte*, 35/36. 34–40.

Reichardt, S. (ed.). (2021). *Die Misstrauensgemeinschaft der "Querdenker"*. Frankfurt am Main: Campus-Verlag.

Renner, K. N. (2020). Facts and Factual Narration in Journalism. In: M. Fludernik & M.-L. Ryan (eds.). *Narrative Factuality. A Handbook*, 465–478. Berlin/Boston: W. de Gruyter.

Rincon, P. (2020). Coronavirus: Is there Any Evidence for Lab Release Theory? *BBC-online*, 01 May 2020.

Rosenberg, A. (1923). *Die Protokolle der Weisen von Zion und die jüdische Weltpolitik*. Munich: Deutscher Volks-Verlag.

Rosenthal, J. (2007). *"Die Ehre des jüdischen Soldaten". Die Judenzählung im ersten Weltkrieg und ihre Folgen*. Frankfurt/M.: Campus.

Rothschild, M. (2021). *The Storm Is Upon Us: How QAnon Became a Movement, Cult and Conspiracy Theory of Everything*. Brooklyn: Melville House.

Sachs, N. (2023). This Will Be a Pyrrhic Victory for Hamas. *The Atlantic*, 7 October 2023. www.theatlantic.com/international/archive/2023/10/israel-war-hamas-attacks/675579/.

Saner, E. (2021). "He was adamant he didn't want it": The Pro-vax Parents with Vaccine-hesitant Kids. *The Guardian*, 4 November 2021.

Schönberger, C. & Schönberger, S. (2023). *Die Reichsbürger. Ermächtigungsversuche einer gespenstischen Bewegung*. Munich: Beck.

Schultheiss, K. (2012). The Dreyfus Affair and History, *Journal of the Historical Society*, 12. 189–203. https://doi.org/10.1111/j.1540-5923.2012.00362.x.

Schumaker, D. (2023). Covid Changed Newt Gingrich's Mind about Health Research Funding. *Politico*, 20 July 2023.

Shermer, M. & Grobman, A. (2000). *Denying History: Who Says the Holocaust Never Happened and Why Do they Say It?* Berkeley: University of California Press.

Simonsen, K. B. (2020). Antisemitism and Conspiracism. In: M. Butter & P. Knight (eds.), *The Routledge Handbook of Conspiracy Theories*, 357–370. London/New York: Routledge.

Slobodian, Q. (2020). How the "great reset" of Capitalism Became an Antilockdown Conspiracy. *The Guardian*, 4 December 2020.

Smith, B. (2023). *The Covid Con: The Global Totalitarians' Secret War Against Humanity*. Bloomington, IN: Trafford Publications.
Smith, D. (2023). "It's just gotten crazy": How the Origins of Covid Became a Toxic US Political Debate. *The Guardian*, 28 February 2023.
SOED (Shorter Oxford Dictionary on Historical Principles). (2002). Eds. W. R. Trumble & A. Stevenson. 2 vols. Oxford: Oxford University Press.
Sperber, D. (1996). *Explaining Culture. A Naturalistic Approach.* Oxford: Blackwell.
Sperber, D. (2000a). An Objection to the Memetic Approach to Culture. In R. Aunger (ed.). *Darwinizing Culture. The Status of Memetics as a Science,* 163–173. Oxford: Oxford University Press.
Sperber, D. (2000b). Metarepresentations in an Evolutionary Perspective. In D. Sperber (ed.). *Metaprepresentations: A Multidisciplinary Perspective*, 117–137. Oxford: Oxford University Press.
Sperber, D., Clément, F., Heintz, C., Mascaro, O., Mercier, H., Origgi, G., & Wilson, D. (2010). Epistemic Vigilance. *Mind & Language*, 25(4). 359–393.
Stack, M. K. (2023). Dr. Fauci Could Have Said a Lot More. *The New York Times*, 28 March 2023.
Stano, S. (2020). The Internet and the Spread of Conspiracy Content. In M. Butter & P. Knight (eds.), *The Routledge Handbook of Conspiracy Theories,* 483–496. London/New York: Routledge.
Stolberg, S. G. & Mueller, B. (2023). Scientists, Under Fire from Republicans, Defend Fauci and Covid Origins Study. *The New York Times*, 11 July 2023.
Subotic, J. (2022). Antisemitism in the Global Populist International. *British Journal of Politics and International Relations,* 24(3). 458–474.
Sunstein, C. R. & Vermeule, A. (2009). Conspiracy Theories: Causes and Cures. *Journal of Political Philosophy* 17(2). 202–227.
T-Online. (2020a). Versuchter Sturm auf den Reichstag hat ein Nachspiel. *T-Online*, 31 August 2020.
T-Online. (2020b). Heilpraktikerin und Gelbwesten lösten Reichstagseklat aus. *T-Online*, 31 August 2020.
Taylor, J. R. (1995). *Linguistic Categorization.* Oxford: Oxford University Press.
Thalmann, K. (2019). *The Stigmatization of Conspiracy Theory since the 1950s: "A Plot to Make Us Look Foolish".* London/New York: Routledge.

The Guardian. (2020). How Coronavirus Has Brought Together Conspiracy Theorists and the Far Right. *The Guardian*, 4 September 2020.

The Hill. (2020). Fauci: It's Mind-boggling that China's Wet Markets Are Still Operating during Coronavirus Pandemic. 3 April 2020. https://thehill.com/changing-america/well-being/prevention-cures/491025-fauci-mind-boggling-that-chinas-wet-markets/.

The Hill. (2021). Trial Ends for Day as Senate Moves to Vote. *The Hill*, 2 December 2021, https://thehill.com/homenews/senate/538594-live-coverage-trump-lawyers-present-defense-focused-on-first-amendment/.

The New York Times. (2020). Far-Right Germans Try to Storm Reichstag as Virus Protests Escalate. *The New York Times*, 31 August 2020.

The New York Times. (2023). Scientists, Under Fire from Republicans, Defend Fauci and Covid Origins Study. *The New York Times*, 11 July 2023.

The Washington Post. (2020a). From "It's going to disappear" to "WE WILL WIN THIS WAR". *The Washington Post*, 31 March 2020.

The Washington Post. (2020b). Fauci Says Fox News Host Jesse Watters Should be Fired for "ambush" and "kill shot" Comments. *The Washington Post*, 14 April 2020.

The Washington Post. (2021). White House Denies Trump Is Considering Firing Fauci Despite His Retweet of a Hashtag Calling for His Ouster. *The Washington Post*, 21 December 2021.

Thießen, M. (2013). Vom immunisierten Volkskörper zum "präventiven Selbst". *Vierteljahreshefte für Zeitgeschichte* 61(1). 35–64. https://doi.org/10.1524/vfzg.2013.0002.

Thorwart, K. (2020). Corona-Demos in Berlin: Von Reichsflagge bis AfD – Eine Fahnenkunde. *Frankfurter Rundschau*, 6 September 2020.

Thorwart, K. (2022). Prinz Reuß von den "Reichsbürgern" bedient antisemitische Verschwörungserzählungen. *Frankfurter Rundschau*, 12 December 2022.

US Attorney's Office. (2022). Man Who Made Threats Against Dr. Anthony Fauci and Other Federal Officials Sentenced to Over Three Years in Federal Prison. U.S. Attorney's Office, District of Maryland, 4 August 2022. www.justice.gov/usao-md/pr/man-who-made-threats-against-dr-anthony-fauci-and-other-federal-officials-sentenced-over#:~:text=Greenbelt%2C%20Maryland%20%E2%80%93%20U.S.%20District%20Judge,sending%20emails%20threatening%20harm%20to.

USA Today. (2022). Fact Check: Video Shows Rep. Jim Jordan question Dr. Anthony Fauci. *USA Today*, 14 November 2022.

Uscinski, J. (2021). *Conspiracy Theories and the People Who Believe Them.* Oxford: Oxford University Press.

Van Dijcke, D. & Wright, A. L. (2021). Profiling Insurrection: Characterizing Collective Action Using Mobile Device Data. Working Paper, Friedmann Institute, University of Chicago. Chicago: The University of Chicago Press.

van Eemeren, F. H. & Grootendorst, R. (1992). *Argumentation, Communication, and Fallacies: A Pragma-dialectical Perspective.* Hillsdale, NJ: Lawrence Erlbaum.

van Eemeren, F. H. & Houtlosser, P. (2002). Strategic Maneuvering with the Burden of Proof. In F. H. van Eemeren (ed.). *Advances in Pragma-Dialectics,* 13–28. Amsterdam/Newport: Sic Sat/Vale Press.

van Eemeren, F. H., Houtlosser, P., & Snoeck Henkemans, F. (2007). *Argumentative Indicators. A Pragma-Dialectical Study.* Dordrecht: Springer.

van Proijen, J.-W. & Douglas, K. (2017). Conspiracy Theories as Part of History: The Role of Societal Crisis Situations. *Memory Studies* 10(3). 323–333. https://doi.org/10.1177/1750698017701615.

van Prooijen, J.-W., Klein, O., & Milošević Đorđević, J. (2020). Social-cognitive Processes Underlying Belief in Conspiracy Theories. In M. Butter & P. Knight (eds.). *The Routledge Handbook of Conspiracy Theories,* 168–180. London: Routledge.

van Prooijen, J.-W. & Imhoff, R. (2022). The Psychological Study of Conspiracy Theories: Strengths and Limitations. *Current Opinion in Psychology* 47.101465. https://doi.org/10.1016/j.copsyc.2022.101465.

van Prooijen, J.-W., Ligthart, J., Rosema, S., & Xu, Y. (2022). The Entertainment Value of Conspiracy Theories. *British Journal of Psychology*, 113. 25–48. https://doi.org/10.1111/bjop.12522.

Wagner, R. & Flannery-Dailey, F. (2005). Wake UP! Worlds of Illusion in Gnosticism, Buddhism and *The Matrix* Project. In C. Grau (ed.). *Philosophers Explore The Matrix.* 258–288. Oxford: Oxford University Press.

Waldman, P. (2021). The Real Reason the Right Hates Anthony Fauci. *The Washington Post,* 21 December 2021.

Walton, D. (2008). *Informal Logic: A Pragmatic Approach.* Cambridge: Cambridge University Press.

Wang, P. & Catalano, T. (2022). Social Media, Right-wing Populism, and Covid-19: A Multimodal Critical Discourse Analysis of Reactions to the "Chinese virus" Discourse. In A. Musoff, R. Breeze,

K. Kondo & S. Vilar-Lluch (eds.). *Pandemic and Crisis Discourse. Communicating Covid-19 and Public Health Strategy,* 321–337. London: Bloomsbury.

Webman, E. (2011). Adoption of the Protocols in the Arab Discourse on the Arab-Israeli Conflict, Zionism and the Jews. In E. Webman (ed.) *The Global Impact of the "Protocols of the Elders of Zion": A Century-old Myth,* 175–195. London: Routledge.

Weiss, D. (2023). Covid-19 Vaccination Policies in an Autocratic Context. How Autocrats Cope with the Corona Challenge: Belarus vs. Russia. In N. Thielemann & D. Weiss (eds.). *Remedies against the Pandemic: How Politicians Communicate their Crisis Management,* 136–168. Amsterdam: John Benjamins.

Wendling, M. (2021). QAnon: What Is It and Where Did It Come from? *BBC,* 6 January 2021. www.bbc.com/news/53498434.

WHO (World Health Organization). (2020a). WHO Director-General's Statement on IHR Emergency Committee on Novel Coronavirus, 22 January 2020. www.who.int/director-general/speeches/detail/who-director-general-s-statement-on-ihr-emergency-committee-on-novel-coronavirus.

WHO (World Health Organization). (2020b). Statement on the Second Meeting of the Emergency Committee Regarding the Outbreak of Novel Coronavirus (2019-NCoV). 30 January 2020. www.who.int/news-room/detail/30-01-2020-statement-on-the-second-meeting-of-the-international-health-regulations-(2005)-emergency-committee-regarding-the-outbreak-of-novel-coronavirus-(2019-ncov).

WHO (World Health Organization). (2024). Number of COVID-19 Deaths Reported to WHO (Cumulative Total). https://data.who.int/dashboards/covid19/deaths.

Whyte, G. (2008). *The Dreyfus Affair: A Chronological History.* Basingstoke/New York: Palgrave Macmillan.

Wilson, D. (2000). Metarepresentation in Linguistic Communication. In D. Sperber (ed.). *Metaprepresentations: A Multidisciplinary Perspective,* 411–448. Oxford: Oxford University Press.

Wippermann, W. (2007). *Agenten des Bösen. Die großen Verschwörungstheorien und was dahinter steckt.* Berlin: Herder.

Wistrich, R. (2010). *A Lethal Obsession. Anti-Semitism from Antiquity to the Global Jihad.* New York: Random House.

Wittmann, R. (ed.) (2021). *Eichmann Trial Reconsidered.* Toronto: University of Toronto Press.

Wodak, R. (2021). Crisis Communication and Crisis Management during COVID-19. *Global Discourse.* https://doi.org/10.1332/2043789 21X16100431230102.

Wong, J. C. (2020). QAnon Explained: The Antisemitic Conspiracy Theory Gaining Traction around the World. *The Guardian*, 25 August 2020. www.theguardian.com/us-news/2020/aug/25/qanon-conspiracy-theory-explained-trump-what-is.

Wood, M. J. & Douglas, K. M. (2013). "What about building 7?" A Social Psychological Study of Online Discussion of 9/11 Conspiracy Theories. *Frontiers in Psychology,* 4. 409.

Yoe, C. (2019). *Principles of Risk Analysis. Decision Making Under Uncertainty.* London/New York: Routledge.

Zipperstein, S. J. (2020). The Conspiracy Theory to Rule Them All. What Explains the Strange, Long Life of The Protocols of the Elders of Zion? *The Atlantic,* 25 August 2020. www.theatlantic.com/politics/archive/2020/08/conspiracy-theory-rule-them-all/615550/.

Zorzi, V. (2022). Collective Identities in the Online Self-representation of Conspiracy Theorists. The Cases of Climate Change Denial, "Deep State" and "Big Pharma". In M. Demata, V. Zorzi & A. Zottola (eds.). *Conspiracy Theory Discourses,* 365–391. Amsterdam: John Benjamins.

Zwierlein, C. & de Graaf, B. (2013). Security and Conspiracy in Modern History. *Historical Social Research* 38(1). 7–45.

Acknowledgments

My thanks go to the colleagues who gave invaluable advice on earlier versions, especially Ingrid Hudabiunigg, Lorella Viola and Daniel Weiss, who read and critiqued the whole ms., as well as to CUP's reviewers who made excellent suggestions for its improvement.

Cambridge Elements

Cognitive Linguistics

Sarah Duffy
Northumbria University

Sarah Duffy is Senior Lecturer in English Language and Linguistics at Northumbria University. She has published primarily on metaphor interpretation and understanding, and her forthcoming monograph for Cambridge University Press (co-authored with Michele Feist) explores *Time, Metaphor, and Language* from a cognitive science perspective. Sarah is Review Editor of the journal, *Language and Cognition*, and Vice President of the UK Cognitive Linguistics Association.

Nick Riches
Newcastle University

Nick Riches is a Senior Lecturer in Speech and Language Pathology at Newcastle University. His work has investigated language and cognitive processes in children and adolescents with autism and developmental language disorders, and he is particularly interested in usage-based accounts of these populations.

Editorial Board

Heng Li, *Southwest University*
John Newman, *University of Alberta (Edmonton)*
Kimberley Pager-McClymont, *University of Huddersfield*
Katie J. Patterson, *Universidad de Granada*
Maria Angeles Ruiz-Moneva, *University of Zaragoza*
Lexi Webster, *Manchester Metropolitan University*
Xu Wen, *Southwest University*

About the Series

Cambridge Elements in Cognitive Linguistics aims to extend the theoretical and methodological boundaries of cognitive linguistics. It will advance and develop established areas of research in the discipline, as well as address areas where it has not traditionally been explored and areas where it has yet to become well-established.

Cambridge Elements

Cognitive Linguistics

Elements in the Series

Navigating the Realities of Metaphor and Psychotherapy Research
Dennis Tay

The Many Faces of Creativity: Exploring Synaesthesia through a Metaphorical Lens
Sarah Turner and Jeannette Littlemore

Metaphor, Metonymy, the Body and the Environment: An Exploration of the Factors That Shape Emotion-Colour Associations and Their Variation across Cultures
Jeannette Littlemore, Marianna Bolognesi, Nina Julich-Warpakowski, Chung-hong Danny Leung and Paula Pérez Sobrino

Applied Cognitive Linguistics and L2 Instruction
Reyes Llopis-García

Cognitive Linguistics and Language Evolution
Michael Pleyer and Stefan Hartmann

Computational Construction Grammar: A Usage-Based Approach
Jonathan Dunn

Signed Language and Cognitive Grammar
Rocío Martínez, Sara Siyavoshi and Sherman Wilcox

Linguistic Synesthesia: A Meta-analysis
Bodo Winter and Francesca Strik-Lievers

Cognition and Conspiracy Theories
Andreas Musolff

A full series listing is available at: www.cambridge.org/ECOG

Printed by Libri Plureos GmbH in Hamburg, Germany